Get Started with Excel 2010

Get Started with Excel 2010

Moira Stephen

For UK order enquiries: please contact Bookpoint Ltd, 130 Milton Park, Abingdon, Oxon OX14 4SB. Telephone: +44 (0) 1235 827720. Fax: +44 (0) 1235 400454. Lines are open 09.00–17.00, Monday to Saturday, with a 24-hour message answering service. Details about our titles and how to order are available at www.teachyourself.com

For USA order enquiries: please contact McGraw-Hill Customer Services, PO Box 545, Blacklick, OH 43004-0545, USA. Telephone: 1-800-722-4726. Fax: 1-614-755-5645.

For Canada order enquiries: please contact McGraw-Hill Ryerson Ltd, 300 Water St, Whitby, Ontario L1N 9B6, Canada. Telephone: 905 430 5000. Fax: 905 430 5020.

Long renowned as the authoritative source for self-guided learning – with more than 50 million copies sold worldwide – the Teach Yourself series includes over 500 titles in the fields of languages, crafts, hobbies, business, computing and education.

British Library Cataloguing in Publication Data: a catalogue record for this title is available from the British Library.

Library of Congress Catalog Card Number: on file.

First published in UK 2010 by Hodder Education, part of Hachette UK, 338 Euston Road, London NW1 3BH.

First published in US 2010 by The McGraw-Hill Companies, Inc.

Previously published as *Teach Yourself Excel 2007*

The Teach Yourself name is a registered trade mark of Hodder Headline.

Typeset by MPS Limited, a Macmillan Company.

Printed in Great Britain for Hodder Education, an Hachette UK Company, 338 Euston Road, London NW1 3BH, by CPI Cox & Wyman, Reading, Berkshire RG1 8EX.

The publisher has used its best endeavours to ensure that the URLs for external websites referred to in this book are correct and active at the time of going to press. However, the publisher and the author have no responsibility for the websites and can make no guarantee that a site will remain live or that the content will remain relevant, decent or appropriate.

Hachette UK's policy is to use papers that are natural, renewable and recyclable products and made from wood grown in sustainable forests. The logging and manufacturing processes are expected to conform to the environmental regulations of the country of origin.

Impression number   10 9 8 7 6 5 4 3 2 1

Year   2014 2013 2012 2011 2010

Front cover: © Nikreates/Alamy

Back cover: © Jakub Semeniuk/iStockphoto.com, © Royalty-Free/Corbis, © agencyby/iStockphoto.com, © Andy Cook/iStockphoto.com, © Christopher Ewing/iStockphoto.com, © zebicho – Fotolia.com, © Geoffrey Holman/iStockphoto.com, © Photodisc/Getty Images, © James C. Pruitt/iStockphoto.com, © Mohamed Saber – Fotolia.com

Contents

Welcome to *Get Started with Excel 2010*

If you need to produce budgets, forecasts, summary data, statistics, financial information, charts or lists of data you'll find all the features you require in Excel.

This book will help you to unleash the power of Excel, quickly and painlessly. We start by introducing the basic skills that are needed to create and format a workbook attractively. Simple formulas and sophisticated formatting options will help to ensure that your worksheets are not only accurate, but look good too!

We then move on to introduce the many different and powerful functions that are available in Excel. Logical, statistical, math, text, date, financial and lookup functions are discussed.

Other features covered include charting and drawing, styles and templates, list management, macros, integration of Excel with other applications, sending worksheets by e-mail and preparing web pages in Excel.

Excel is a very powerful spreadsheet package – but don't let that put you off. You'll be amazed at what can be achieved easily!

I hope that you enjoy using this book and that it helps you to learn to use Excel.

Moira Stephen

Only got a minute?

OK. You need to learn how to use Excel – but you are *really* short on time. And you're really not sure where you should start and what you need to know.

Well, Excel is excellent when it comes to displaying your data in a table format, and at enabling you to perform calculations on it or to summarise it. And you don't need to be a mathematical or financial genius to get it to do something useful!

If you have never used Excel before and/or are new to the Office 2010 interface – take a look through Chapter 1 before you start. Even if Excel is already installed on your computer, a quick flick through this chapter will introduce the Office 2010 interface and some of the terms – e.g. Ribbon, groups, Quick Access toolbar – that you need to know, regardless of what Office application you are using.

Move on to Chapter 2 to get the essential Excel skills – and experiment with what is there – you'll even be able to create simple formulas by the time you reach the end of this chapter.

Chapter 3 will give you suggestions that will help you lay out your worksheet attractively – using a selection of formatting and presentation techniques. It also introduces some handy features for when your worksheet gets bigger – things like freeze panes and split screen – so that you can see bits of your worksheet that don't normally all fit on the screen together at the same time.

And Chapter 5 will get you started on functions – the ones that are almost universally useful – for example those used to total a group of cells, or return the minimum, maximum or average value from a range of cells.

So if you are starting from scratch, and don't have much time to spend learning Excel, you don't have to tackle the whole book at once – Chapters 1, 2, 3 and 5 might even give you as much as you need.

Use Excel to create something that you need to do – sort out your personal finances, record the PTA income and expenditure, budget for your holiday – then you can really start to appreciate what it can do for you, and get on top of things from day 1.

5 Only got five minutes?

The fact that you are reading this suggests that you are looking for something to help you make better use of Excel. You might be new to Excel, or use it a bit but feel that there is more potential in it than you have realised.

You don't want a huge volume to plough through – they look too intimidating and time consuming. And you want something in plain English – because computer speak just isn't really your language! So this book has caught your eye.

The essentials are really covered in: -

Chapter 1: Getting Started
Chapter 2: Basic Excel Skills
Chapter 3: Formatting and Layout
Chapter 5: Formulas and Functions

So if you are new or relatively new to Excel – take a look at them first.

You can develop your basic skills further in the other chapters.

In Chapter 4 you will learn how to add, remove, copy and move worksheets – and rename them so you can quickly identify which sheet you want to go to. It also looks at features that will help you lay out your sheets more consistently by using themes, or speed up the input of standard data and formulas by grouping.

Chapter 6 introduces a range of different types of functions – demonstrating that Excel can be used for much more than basic statistical work.

Everyone loves the charting features in Excel – used to display your data diagrammatically – and useful for showing trends and how one set of data relates to another. Take a look at Chapter 7 if this is something that you would like to be able to do.

Chapter 8 shows you how templates and styles can make your workbooks look more professional, and speed up creating and formatting workbooks. Templates can store the standard text, logos, layout, functions and styles required in your workbook. The styles store the formatting that you want to apply to your cells. Whether you are using Excel to at your work, or to keep the books for any other group – your golf club or horticultural club – you can give all your worksheets a more consistent look and feel by using templates and styles.

Excel contains some pretty powerful database features – allowing you to sort, filter and extract data from a list. These features are covered in Chapter 9. If your database needs are more sophisticated than Excel can handle, there is always Access (but that's another book).

Chapters 10 introduces Macros – giving you a way store a sequence of commands or routines that you perform repetitively – and then run them at the click of a button! I like this feature when inserting some headers and footers in workbooks.

Excel is only one application in Office 2010 – and it integrates very well with the other applications. Chapter 11 discusses some of the ways that you can work across those applications with Excel.

And finally Chapter 12 looks at using Excel with the wider world – through email, fax and the Web.

So Excel has lots of potential – and this book will help you on your way to realising how you can make the most of its potential.

At the end of each chapter you'll find a quick test – so you can check how much you have learnt. And, if necessary, you can go back and work through a section again to help improve your understanding.

You will also find 50 interactive questions on line – so you can set yourself a challenge and try them out once you think you have mastered the book!

You may already be working towards an IT user qualification. If you aren't you might enjoy the challenge of working towards a qualification. If you would like a formal User IT qualification you could consider

European Computer Driving Licence (ECDL)
(http://www.bcs.org/server.php?show=nav.5829)

British Computer Society (BCS) IT User qualifications
(http://www.bcs.org/server.php?show=nav.7784)

Scottish Qualification Authority (SQA) units
(http://www.sqa.org.uk/sqa/CCC_FirstPage.jsp)

This book covers most of the features examined in the qualifications listed – at Level 1, 2 and 3.

Whatever your goal, good luck – and I hope you find this book supports you in your endeavours.

Getting started

In this chapter you will learn:
- **what you need to run Excel 2010**
- **how to install the software**
- **how to start Excel**
- **about the Excel screen and its tools**
- **how to use the Help system**

1.1 Introducing Excel

Excel is a very powerful spreadsheet package – but don't let that put you off! You can use Excel to produce simple spreadsheets to help you prepare your invoices, budgets and summary statements. You can also use Excel to chart your data, manipulate it using database-type features and publish your worksheet to the Web. Excel integrates well with the other packages in Microsoft Office and you'll find out how you can use this to your advantage. Finally, Excel is very web-orientated – you'll soon be able to hyperlink to other files and Internet addresses, send e-mails and publish your worksheets and charts on the Web!

It is assumed that you have a working knowledge of Windows 7.

Excel 2010 is included in all of the Office 2010 suites.

1.2 System requirements

These hardware and software specifications are for Office 2010.
Hardware that is capable of running Office 2007 will support
Office 2010. The recommended configuration is a PC with a
minimum of a 500 MHz processor, 256 MB of RAM and 1.5 GB
disk space. The minimum specification is given in the table below.

Processor	500 MHz or higher
Memory	256 MB RAM or higher
Hard disk	1.5 GB. A portion of this will be freed after installation if the installation files are removed from the hard drive.
Display	1024 × 768 or higher resolution monitor
Operating system	Windows XP with Service Pack (SP) 3 (32-bit operating system (OS) only) or Windows Vista with SP1, Windows 7, Windows Server 2003 R2 with MSXML 6.0, Windows Server 2008, or later 32- or 64-bit OS.
Additional	Requirements and product functionality can vary based on the system configuration and operating system.
Graphics Processor	Use of graphics hardware acceleration requires DirectX 9.0c compatible graphics card with 64 MB or higher video memory (optional to help speed up some graphics features in Office 2010)
Browser	Internet Explorer 6.0 or later, 32-bit browser only.

1.3 Installing Excel

To install Microsoft Office, follow the on-screen instructions.

1 Insert the CD into the CD drive. The CD will launch
   automatically, and the setup begin.

2 At the **Setup** dialog box, enter the 25-character product key.

3 For the user information, enter your name, initials (optional) and organization (optional). Your name will be used in the **Author** box in the **Properties** dialog box in the Office programs.

4 Read the End-User License Agreement and select **I accept the terms ...** (if you don't agree, you can't continue!).

5 Select the type of installation.

6 At the final Setup stage, select the options and you're done!

1.4 Starting Excel

1 Click the **Start** button on the Taskbar.

2 Point to **All Programs**.

3 Select Microsoft Office.

4 Click **Microsoft Office Excel 2010**.

1.5 The Excel screen

When Excel starts, you are presented with a new workbook displaying a blank worksheet. We'll take a tour of the Excel screen, so that you know what the various areas are called. You'll find the different screen areas referred to by the names given below in the on-line Help and throughout this book.

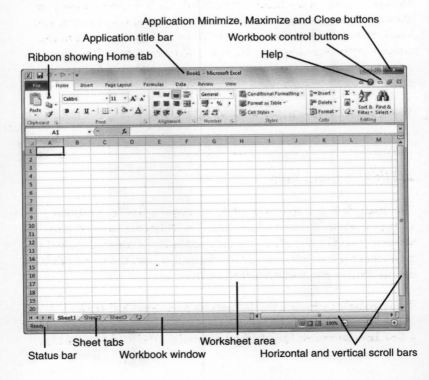

Application Minimize, Maximize and Close buttons

Application title bar

Workbook control buttons

Ribbon showing Home tab

Help

Status bar

Sheet tabs

Workbook window

Worksheet area

Horizontal and vertical scroll bars

If the workbook window is maximized, the workbook and the application windows share one title bar containing the application and workbook names.

1.6 Workbooks and worksheets

When working in Excel, the files that you create and work with are called workbooks. Each workbook consists of a number of worksheets – the default number is three. A worksheet is the primary document, and consists of cells organized into rows and columns. You can add, delete, move, copy and rename the worksheets, depending on your work requirements.

Related data is usually best kept on separate worksheets within the same workbook – this makes it easier to find and manage your data. For example, if you were collating regional sales figures, you could record the figures for each region on a separate sheet in the same workbook. Alternatively, you could have a workbook for each region and record the monthly or quarterly sales figures on separate sheets in each region's workbook.

Worksheets will be discussed more fully in Chapter 4.

1.7 Ribbon and tabs

The Excel features and commands are displayed on the Ribbon along the top of the worksheet area. The Ribbon is divided into task-orientated tabs, where the commands and features required to perform different tasks are grouped together, e.g. the Insert tab has all the objects you might want to insert.

You can hide or restore the Ribbon by pressing [Ctrl]-[F1].

Click any tab to display it temporarily when the Ribbon is hidden.

Program tabs replace the standard tabs when you perform certain tasks, e.g. Print Preview.

GROUPS AND COMMAND BUTTONS

The command buttons on each tab are arranged in groups, e.g. the Insert tab has all the command buttons grouped together into areas – Tables, Illustrations, Charts, Sparklines, Filter, Links, Text and Symbols.

BACKSTAGE VIEW

When you click **File** (at the top left of the Ribbon) you are taken into Backstage view.

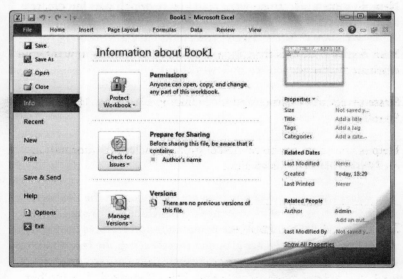

Backstage view displays six buttons and six tabs. The buttons are used to:

▶ Save, open and close a file

- Display and edit Excel options – you can customize your Excel settings, e.g. the default place to save workbooks, the default number of recent files to display on the Recent list. Explore the options to see the kind of things you can specify.
- Exit the application.

The tabs are:

Info gives information about the current workbook.

Recent shows a list of recently-used workbooks. The default number of files to list here is 20. You can *pin* a file to this list by clicking the pin icon to the right of the workbook name – this ensures that is doesn't disappear off the list (the pin is a toggle, click it again to release the workbook).

New presents a selection of templates from which you can create a new workbook.

Print displays options that allow you to specify how you want your worksheet printed.

Share reveals file-sharing options including e-mail, SkyDrive and SharePoint.

Help is your gateway to the Excel support including information on **What's New** in this version.

1.8 Quick Access toolbar

The Quick Access toolbar contains commands that are regularly used, and are independent of the tab being displayed. The toolbar can be displayed in one of two positions:

1 Above the Ribbon, beside the Microsoft Office button (the default position).

2 Below the Ribbon.

To move the Quick Access toolbar from one position to the other, click the arrow at its right and select **Place**

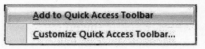

Quick Access Toolbar below the Ribbon or **Place Quick Access Toolbar above the Ribbon** as required.

Author's insight

You can customize the Quick Access toolbar in the Excel Options dialog box.

Click the arrow at the end of the toolbar and select **More Commands...**

You can also add a command to the Quick Access toolbar directly from the Ribbon.

1 Right-click on the command you wish to add.
2 Click on **Add to Quick Access Toolbar.**

(Remove a command from the toolbar in the same way –
right-click on it and choose **Remove from Quick Access
Toolbar**).

1.9 Dialog box launchers

Dialog box launchers are small buttons that
appear at the bottom right of some groups.

Clicking a launcher opens a dialog box that
displays more options related to the group.

Dialog box launcher

1.10 Ribbon keyboard shortcuts

If you prefer to issue commands using the keyboard, Excel will
automatically prompt you as you work.

1 Hold down [**Enter**] – and keep it down throughout the procedure.
A 'ghost' letter appears next to each tab on the Ribbon.
2 Press the letter key to activate the tab you want to use. Ghost
letters/numbers will appear next to each command.
3 Press the letter/number to select the command button.
4 Release [**Enter**].

1.11 Help

As you work with Excel you will probably find that you need
Help from time to time. To access the Help system:

Click the **Help** button to the right of the Ribbon tabs.

Or
▶ Press [F1].

To browse through the Help pages, click on any feature in the
Help window.

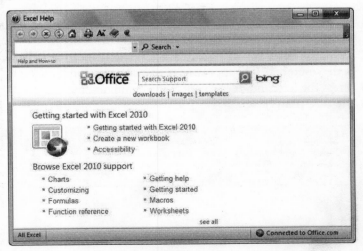

Use the Help toolbar as you work in the Help pages.

Back Stop Home Change Font Size Keep on top/Not on top

Forward Refresh Print Show/hide Table of Contents

To search for Help on a topic:

1 Enter details of what you are looking for in the Search field.
2 Click **Search**.

Or

3 Click the search drop-down arrow and select a search area.

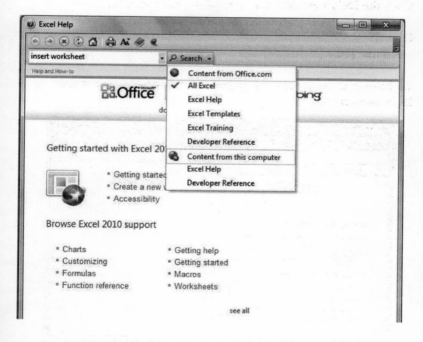

1.12 Exiting Excel

When you have finished working in Excel you must close the application down – don't just switch off your computer.

To exit Excel:
1. Click the **Close** button in the right-hand corner of the application title bar.

Or

2. Click **File** to go to Backstage view and then click **Exit**.

THINGS TO REMEMBER

1 *You can start Excel from the Start menu or a desktop icon.*

2 *An Excel file is known as a workbook and may contain any number of worksheets.*

3 *Almost all the commands can be reached through the Ribbon, where they are grouped in tabs.*

4 *The filing commands are reached through Backstage view.*

5 *Commands can be added to the Quick Access toolbar for one-click access.*

6 *Some options are held in dialog boxes. To see these, click the launcher for the group.*

7 *You can choose commands from the Ribbon using the keyboard.*

8 *Excel has a very comprehensive Help system.*

9 *To exit Excel, close the window or use File > Exit.*

TEST

1 *Identify the following parts on the diagram*
   ▷ *Worksheet area*
   ▷ *Worksheet tabs*
   ▷ *Ribbon*
   ▷ *Status bar*
   ▷ *Title bar*
   ▷ *Help button*
   ▷ *Formulas tab*
   ▷ *Dialog box launcher*
   ▷ *Quick Access toolbar*

2 *What are the keyboard shortcuts to:*
   i *Toggle the display of the Ribbon*
   ii *Open the Help system.*

2

....

Basic Excel skills

In this chapter you will learn:
- *some spreadsheet jargon*
- *about workbooks*
- *about entering and editing text, data and formulas*
- *about formatting cells*
- *how to move and copy data and formulas*

2.1 Spreadsheet jargon

This chapter will introduce you to the basic skills you will need to work in Excel. By the time you have completed this chapter you will have created a simple worksheet and you will know how to create, edit, save, print, open and close a workbook.

Before going any further, spend a little time getting familiar with some of the jargon you will encounter. There's nothing difficult about it – once you know what it means!

ROWS, COLUMNS AND CELLS

The worksheet area consists of rows, columns and cells. Rows are identified by the numbers down the left side of the worksheet area. Row 7 is highlighted in the illustration below.

Columns are identified by letters displayed along the top of the worksheet area. Column E is highlighted in the illustration.

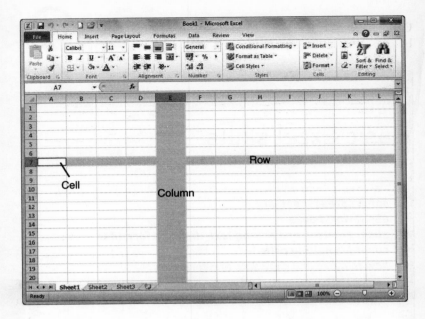

Where a row and column intersect you have a cell. Each of the rectangular areas on your worksheet is a cell. Cells are identified using a cell name or address. A cell address consists of the column letter followed by the number of the row that intersects it to create the cell.

Excel vital statistics

Number of rows in a worksheet: 1,048,576

Number of columns in a worksheet: 16,384 – columns A to XFD.

Last cell on a worksheet: XFD1048576

Number of sheets in a workbook: the default is 3, limited by the memory of your computer

Undo limit: 100

See **Excel specifications and limits** in the online Help for full details.

Cell A1, B9, C3, D6 and F3 have been highlighted in the screenshot below.

TEXT, DATA, FORMULAS AND FUNCTIONS

The cells in your worksheet will eventually contain text, numeric data, formulas or functions.

Text is used for titles or narrative to describe the figures that you are presenting. Worksheet headings, column headings and row labels will usually be text entries.

Numeric data means the figures that appear in your worksheet. The data may be entered through the keyboard, or it may be generated as the result of a calculation.

Formulas are used to perform calculations on the numeric data in your worksheet (see section 2.10 and Chapter 5). Formulas are used to add the value in one cell to that in another or multiply the values in different cells, etc. Some of your formulas will be very basic while others may be quite complex.

Functions are predefined formulas that perform simple or complex calculations (see Chapters 5 and 6). There are many different kinds of functions set up in Excel – statistical, logical, financial, database, engineering – and many more. You're bound to find some useful ones, whatever type of data you work with.

2.2 File handling

In Excel, a file is called a workbook. Each new workbook you create is automatically given a temporary filename – Book1, Book2, etc. The name appears on the workbook title bar.

When you open Excel a new workbook is created automatically. There are several ways in which you can create new workbooks and open existing ones in Excel.

NEW WORKBOOK

To create a new blank workbook:
- Click **New** on the **Quick Access Toolbar** (if you have added the command to it).

Or
- Press [Ctrl]-[N].

To create a workbook based on a workbook or template:
1 Click **File** to display Backstage view.
2 Select **New**.

3 Choose **New from existing** to create a workbook based on an existing file.

Or

- Select the **template** that you want to create a workbook from and click **Create** (if the template is stored locally) or **Download** (if you have selected one from Office.com).

OPEN A WORKBOOK

To open an existing workbook:

1 Click **Open** on the **Quick Access Toolbar** (if you have added the command to it).

Or

- Press [**Ctrl**]-[**O**].

Open

2 Locate and select the file required.

3 Click **Open**.

To open a recently used file:

1 Click **File** to display Backstage view.

2 Select **Recent**.

3 Click on the file required in the **Recent Workbooks** list.

SAVE A WORKBOOK

At some stage you must save your workbook to disk (if you don't you will lose it when you switch off your computer). When you save your workbook, you should give it a filename that reflects its contents rather than use the *Bookx* temporary name.

You can save your workbook at any time – you don't need to wait until you've entered all your data. I suggest you save your workbook regularly – and remember to resave it when you make changes to it. If you haven't saved your workbook, and your computer crashes or you have a power failure, you may lose any unsaved data.

To save your workbook:

1 Click **Save** on the Quick Access Toolbar (or press **[Ctrl]-[S]** or choose **Save** in Backstage view).

Save

2 At the **Save As** dialog box, locate the folder into which you wish to save your workbook (usually Documents or a sub-folder).

3 Enter the name in the **File name:** field.

4 Leave the **Save as type:** at **Excel Workbook**.

5 Click **Save**.

You are returned to your workbook. Its name appears on the workbook title bar.

Once the workbook has been saved you can save your changes to it whenever you wish.

- Click **Save** on the Quick Access toolbar or press **[Ctrl]-[S]**, or choose **Save** in Backstage view. The **Save As** dialog box does not reappear, but the up-to-date version of your workbook replaces the old one saved to disk.

Save As...

There may be times when you save a workbook, then edit it, and then decide that you want to save the edited version of the workbook **and** keep the original version too.

If you don't want to overwrite the original with the updated version, click the **File** tab to go into Backstage view choose **Save As...** to display the **Save As** dialog box again.

You can select a different folder and/or filename for the new version of the file.

The keyboard shortcut for **Save As...** is [**F12**].

PASSWORD PROTECTION

If you wish to password protect your workbook (so that no one can open or edit the workbook unless they know the password) you can do so from the **Save As** dialog box.

1 Click **Tools** at the bottom of the **Save As** dialog box.
2 Choose **General Options...**
3 Enter the **password**(s) and click **OK**.
4 Re-enter the password(s) at the prompt.
5 Click **OK**.

CLOSE WORKBOOK

- Click **Close** in Backstage view.

Or

- Click **Close window** (to the right of the ribbon tabs).

2.3 Moving around your worksheet

Before you can enter anything into a cell, you must make the cell you want to work on active. To make a single cell active, you must select it. You can easily move onto any cell (thus making it active) using either the keyboard or the mouse.

The active cell has a dark border. The address of the active cell appears in the Name box to the left of the formula bar.

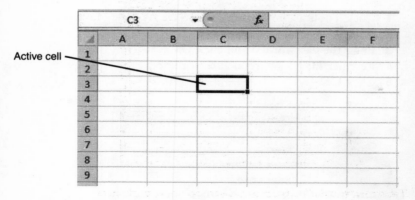

Active cell

To make a cell active
Using the mouse

- Click on the cell (you may need to use the horizontal or vertical scrollbars to bring it into view).

Using the keyboard

- Use the right, left, up and down arrow keys to move right or left one column, or up or down one row at a time.
- Hold down [Ctrl] and press an arrow key to move to the last occupied cell in that direction.
- Press [Enter] to move onto the cell directly below the one that is currently active.

You can also go to a specific cell, if you know its address.

To go to a specific cell:
- Type the cell address into the **Name** box and press [Enter].

Or
1 Press [F5].
2 Enter the address of the cell you want to go to in the **Reference** field of the **Go To** dialog box.
3 Click **OK**.

To return to cell A1 from anywhere in your worksheet:
- Hold down [Ctrl] and press [Home].

To move to the end of the work area on your worksheet (the last cell you have worked on, rather than cell XFD1048576):
- Hold down [Ctrl] and press [End].

Check out **Keyboard shortcuts** in the on-line Help to see if there are any others that you would find useful.

2.4 Selection techniques

You will often work on more than one cell at a time in Excel. You may need to format a group of cells in a particular way or copy or move a group, or apply a function to a group.

A group of cells is called a cell range. Ranges of adjacent cells are identified by the first cell address in the range, then a colon, followed by the last cell address, e.g. A1:A7, C3:D12; F5:H7. These ranges are highlighted below. Non-adjacent cell ranges have the cell addresses separated by commas.

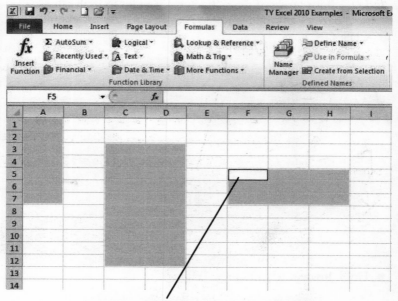

Note that the first cell selected is not highlighted

USING THE MOUSE

To select a group of adjacent cells:

- Click and drag over the range of cells you wish to select.

Or

1 Click on a cell at one corner of the range you wish to select.
2 Hold down [Shift].
3 Click on the cell in the diagonally opposite corner of the range you want to select.

To select a row or rows:

- Click the number to the left of the row you want to select.

Or

- Drag down over the row numbers to select several rows.

To select a column or columns:

- Click the letter at the top of the column you want to select.

Or

- Drag across the column letters to select several columns.

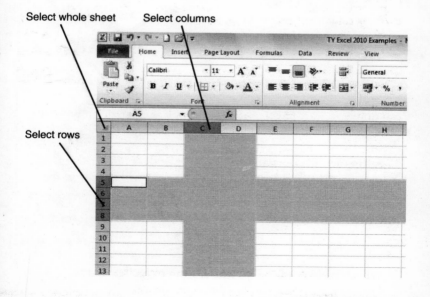

To select the whole worksheet:
- Click the box at the far left of the column letters.

To select a range of non-adjacent cells:
1. Click on one of the cells you want to select.
2. Hold down [Ctrl].
3. Click on each of the other cells you want to select.

To deselect a range of cells:
- Click on any cell outside the range.

USING THE KEYBOARD

To select a group of adjacent cells:
1. Click in a cell at the corner of the range you wish to select.
2. Hold down [Shift].
3. Press the arrow keys to move to the cell in the corner diagonally opposite, and release [Shift].

To deselect a range of cells:
- Press one of the arrow keys.

2.5 Entering text and numeric data

Each time you start Excel a new workbook is created. Entering text or data into your worksheet is easy.

1. Select the cell you want to enter text or data into.
2. Type in the text or data – the text or data will appear in the Formula bar as well as in the active cell.

3. Press [Enter] or click the 'tick' button to the left of the Formula bar when you've completed the cell.

The spreadsheet shown contains:

	A	B	C	D	E	F	G
1	Sales Figures 1st Quarter						
2							
3	Firt name	Surname	January	February	March	Total	
4	Ann	Burns	75000	52000	45000	2E+05	
5	Robert	Donaldsor	60000	65000	56000	2E+05	
6	Gill	McKenzie	55000	70000	65000	2E+05	
7	Jackie	Munro	86000	65000	75000	2E+05	
8	Jim	Andrews	90000	82000	80000	3E+05	
9	Total		366000	334000	321000	1E+06	
10							
11							

Author's insight

Things to note when entering numeric data:

- If a number won't fit in the cell, an Exp message or ###### is displayed.
- Numbers align by default to the right (see section 3.2).

Things to note when entering text:

- Text that doesn't fit into a single cell will 'spill over' into the cell to the right if that one is empty.
- Text that doesn't fit into a single cell will be only partially displayed if the cell to the right is not empty. You will need to widen the column (see section 2.7) to display all of the text.
- Text aligns by default to the left of a cell (see section 3.2).

2.6 Editing text and numeric data

If you make an error when entering data, you can fix things by:

▶ *Deleting the contents of the cell.*
▶ *Replacing the contents of the cell.*
▶ *Editing the contents of the cell.*

To delete the contents of a cell (or cells):
  1 Select the cell (or cells) whose contents you want to erase.
  2 Press [**Delete**].

To replace all the contents of a cell:
  1 Select the cell whose contents you want to replace.
  2 Type in the text or data that should be in the cell.

To edit the contents of a cell:
  1 Select the cell whose contents you want to edit.
  2 Click in the Formula bar.
  3 Edit the cell contents as required (move right and left using the arrow keys, delete characters using [**Delete**] or [**Backspace**], or enter text or data through the keyboard).
  4 Press [**Enter**] when you've finished editing to return to the worksheet.
Or
  1 Double-click in the cell whose contents you want to edit – this places the insertion point within the cell.
  2 Edit the cell contents as required.
  3 Press [**Enter**] when you've finished editing.

Examples in this book

In this book we will use several worksheets to illustrate various features of Excel. I suggest you enter these examples into a workbook and use them as practice material. You can then follow the instructions and experiment with the features.

Simon's Sports

The first worksheet will display a list of items that are in a sale in Simon's Sports. Enter the text displayed in the worksheet below and build up the worksheet as you work through the rest of the chapter.

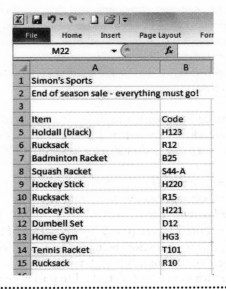

2.7 Column width

If the text you are entering into a cell is more than the column width will accommodate, you must do something about it if you want it to be fully visible.

Sometimes – particularly with main headings at the top of a worksheet – it doesn't matter if the text spills over into the cells to the right. However, when entering column headings or row labels each entry should occupy a single cell – with no overspill into the next column.

One way to make text fit into a single cell is to adjust the width of the column.

MANUAL ADJUSTMENT

To change the width of a column:
- In the column heading row, click and drag the vertical line to the right of the column whose width you want to change – in this example we need to widen column A.

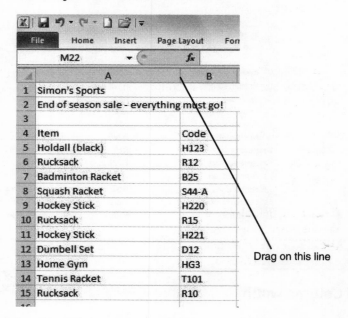

Drag on this line

To set a column to a specific width:
1 Select any cell in the column you want to adjust.
2 Display the **Home** tab on the Ribbon.
3 Click the **Format** button on the Cells group.
4 Select **Column Width...**

5 Complete the **Column Width** dialog box – the value is the number of characters that will fit in the standard font.

6 Click **OK**.

To change the column width to fit the contents:
1 Select the cell that will determine the width of your column.
2 Click the **Format** button on the **Cells** group.
3 Choose **AutoFit Selection**.

■ You can quickly format all column widths to automatically fit – click the **Select All** button – then double-click any boundary between the column headings.

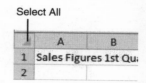

To change the default width for all columns:
1 Select the worksheet – click on its tab.

Or

■ To set the default for the whole workbook – right-click on a sheet tab and click **Select All Sheets**.

2 Click the **Format** button on the Cells group.
3 Select **Default Width...**
4 Enter the width required and click **OK**.

	A	B	C	D	E
1	Simon's Sports				
2	End of season sale - everything must go!				
3					
4	Item	Code	Recommended Retail Price	Sale Price	Saving
5	Holdall (black)	H123			
6	Rucksack	R12			
7	Badminton Racket	B25			

J15 f_x

Column heading with **Wrap text** turned on

AUTOFIT

You can get Excel to automatically adjust the width of the column to fit the entries within it.

To adjust the column width automatically:
■ In the column heading row, double-click the vertical line to the right of the column you want to adjust.

2.8 Other text cell formatting options

WRAP TEXT

To specify that text should wrap within a cell:
1 Select the cells you want to set the text wrap option for.
2 On the **Home** tab, click the **Wrap text** tool in the **Alignment** group.

You will find other options in the **Format Cells** dialog box.

■ To open the dialog box, click the **Format** button in the **Cells** group, and choose **Format Cells...** from the options.

Experiment with the other options to see what effect they have

TEXT ROTATION

To rotate text within a cell:
1 Select the cell(s).
2 Click the **Orientation** tool in the **Alignment** group on the **Home** tab.
3 Select a text orientation from the options.

SHRINK TO FIT

If the contents of a cell are a little too wide for the column width, and you don't want to widen the column, you can get the contents of the cell to 'shrink to fit'.

1 Select the cell whose contents you want to shrink to fit.
2 Click the **Format** button in the **Cells** group on the **Home** tab, and select **Format Cells...** from the options.
3 On the **Alignment** tab, select the **Shrink to fit** checkbox and click **OK**.

2.9 Number formats

Much of the data entered into worksheets is currency. Most of the time that you have a currency value, you will want the appropriate symbol to precede the value – the £, € or other currency symbol.

To place a currency symbol in front of a figure:
■ Format the cells to display the entry in a currency format.
Or
■ Enter the symbol through the keyboard.

If you enter your figures through the numeric keypad, it's probably easiest to format the cells to display the figures as currency.

You can format cells before or after you have entered your text or data.

To format the cells to display the figures in currency format:

1 Select the cells you want to format (see section 2.4 above)
2 Click the currency button in the **Number** group on the **Home** tab if you want the £ symbol, or click the drop-down arrow on this button and select the symbol required.

£ English (U.K.)

$ English (U.S.)

€ Euro (€ 123)

More Accounting Formats...

The Number group has some other buttons to help you format numbers – Percent style, Comma style, Increase and Decrease decimal (these two change the number of decimal places displayed). Other number formats can be found on the Number tab in the Format Cells dialog box – have a look to see if any would be useful.

To apply a format from the **Format Cells** dialog box:
1 Select the cells you want to format.
2 Click the **Format** button in the **Cells** group then click **Format Cells…**
3 Select the **Number** tab in the **Format Cells** dialog box.
4 Choose a category from the list.
5 Complete the dialog box as required – exactly what appears in it depends on the category you select.
6 Click **OK**.

	A	B	C	D	E
1	Simon's Sports				
2	End of season sale - everything must go!				
3					
4	Item	Code	Recommended Retail Price	Sale Price	Saving
5	Holdall (black)	H123	£ 15.50	£ 9.99	
6	Rucksack	R12	£ 16.99	£ 9.99	
7	Badminton Racket	B25	£ 24.00	£ 15.99	
8	Squash Racket	S44-A	£ 27.75	£ 19.99	
9	Hockey Stick	H220	£ 16.99	£ 9.99	
10	Rucksack	R15	£ 40.00	£ 29.99	
11	Hockey Stick	H221	£ 18.99	£ 10.99	
12	Dumbell Set	D12	£ 36.99	£ 24.00	
13	Home Gym	HG3	£ 245.99	£175.00	
14	Tennis Racket	T101	£ 36.99	£ 25.99	
15	Rucksack	R10	£ 7.99	£ 5.49	

2.10 Formulas

Any cell in your workbook, which will contain a figure that has been calculated using other entries in your workbook, should have a formula or function in it (do not do your calculations on a calculator, then type the answer into your workbook).

Formulas allow you to add, subtract, multiply, divide and work out percentages of the values in cells.

Things to note about formulas

Operators used in formulas are:

+	Add	-	Subtract
/	Divide	*	Multiply
%	Percentage		

Formulas start with an equal sign (=)

In our example we are going to use a formula to work out how much a customer will save if they buy something out of the sale.

To work out the saving for the first item in the list (the holdall), we need to subtract the sale price (the figure in cell D6) from the recommended retail price (in cell C6). The result of this calculation should be displayed in cell E6, in the Saving column.

To enter the formula:
  1 Select the cell that will contain the result of the calculation (E6 in this example).
  2 Press the [=] key on your keyboard (to tell Excel we're entering a formula).
  3 Click on cell C6 (the retail price cell for the item).
  ■ The cell address appears in the formula bar and in the current cell.
  4 Press the [-] key on your keyboard (we're subtracting).
  5 Click on cell D6 (the cell containing the sale price figure).
  6 Press [Enter]. The result will appear in cell E6.

At step 3 and step 5, I suggested you click on the cell you want to use in a formula. If you prefer, you can enter the cell address manually by typing the coordinates into your formula instead.

	A	B	C	D	E
1	Simon's Sports				
2					
3	End of season sale - everything must go!				
4					
5	Item	Code	Recommended Retail Price	Sale Price	Saving
6	Holdall (black)	H123	£ 15.50	£ 9.99	=C6-D6
7	Rucksack	R12	£ 16.99	£ 9.99	
8	Badminton Racket	B25	£ 24.00	£ 15.99	
9	Squash Racket	S44-A	£ 27.75	£ 19.99	
10	Hockey Stick	H220	£ 16.99	£ 9.99	
11	Rucksack	R15	£ 40.00	£ 29.99	
12	Hockey Stick	H221	£ 18.99	£ 10.99	
13	Dumbell Set	D12	£ 36.99	£ 24.00	
14	Home Gym	HG3	£ 245.99	£175.00	
15	Tennis Racket	T101	£ 36.99	£ 25.99	
16	Rucksack	R10	£ 7.99	£ 5.49	

SIMPLE FORMULA EXAMPLES

=A7/B6	Divide the figure in A7 by the figure in B6
=D22*12	Multiply the figure in D22 by 12
=C7*25%	Calculate 25% of the figure in C7

Order of precedence

If there is a mixture of operators in a formula, Excel will deal with the multiplication and division before it deals with the addition and subtraction.

=A4+C7*D7

Multiply the figure in C7 by the one in D7, and add the answer to the figure in A4.

=A1+B2/C3+D4*E5-F2

Add to the figure in A1, the result of dividing the figure in B2 by that in C3, then add the result of multiplying the figure in D4 by that in E5, then subtract the figure in F2.

Parentheses

Formulas can become quite long and complicated – and tricky to follow! If you want to force the order in which a formula is calculated, or make a long one easier to read, use parentheses ( ). In the example below, the calculation in each set of parentheses is solved before working through the formula – and the result is different from the formula without parentheses.

=(A1+B2)/C3+(D4*(E5-F2))

Add A1 to B2   we'll call this AB
Subtract F2 from E5   we'll call this FE
Multiply D4 by FE   we'll call this DF

To get the final result:

Divide AB by C3 then add DF.

To help you remember this, think BODMAS! Brackets first, then Division and Multiplication, and then Addition and Subtraction. Always work left to right and never move the position of the entries you are calculating.

2.11 AutoFill

In Simon's Sports sale worksheet, we could work down the column entering the formula for each Saving cell as described in section 2.10. However, a much quicker way to achieve the same result is to use AutoFill. This allows you to copy a formula from one cell into adjacent cells – to the right, left, up or down.

To AutoFill the formula in E6 to the other Saving cells:
1 Select E6.
2 Position the pointer over the bottom right corner of the cell – the Fill Handle (a small black cross) should appear.
3 Click and drag the cross down over the other Saving cells (or double-click the Fill Handle).

When you release the mouse, the formula in cell E6 will be copied to the cells you dragged over.

If you click on each cell in the saving column and keep an eye on the Formula bar, you will notice that Excel has automatically changed the cell addresses in the formula relative to the position you have copied the formula to. Neat trick!

When you AutoFill text or data, a Smart tag appears below the data that you have copied. Click the Smart tag to see the AutoFill options. If you don't want the default, click the option required.

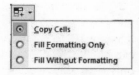

■ Once a formula has been copied into a cell, as in column E in this example, it will extend down the column automatically

as you add new rows! If you type in another item in row 17, the
formula in row 16 will copy to row 17 once the required data is
entered. Try adding some data and watch what happens!

Hockey Stick	H220	£ 16.99	£ 9.99
Rucksack	R15	£ 40.00	£ 29.99
Hockey Stick	H221	£ 18.99	£ 10.99
Dumbell Set	D12	£ 36.99	£ 24.00
Home Gym	HG3	£ 245.99	£ 175.00
Tennis Racket	T101	£ 36.99	£ 25.99
Rucksack	R10	£ 7.99	£ 5.49

AUTOFILLING DATES AND NUMBERS

AutoFill can be a real time-saver in some situations. Try this:

To enter column or row labels for each month of the year or day of
the week:
1 Enter the first month or day you want to use into the
   appropriate cell – January or Jan, September or Sept,
   Wednesday or Wed.
2 AutoFill the contents of that cell across the columns or down
   the rows.
■ Excel will automatically complete the other cells.

To enter a row or column of numbers in sequence, e.g. 1, 2, 3, 4
etc. or 50, 100, 150 etc.:
1 Enter the first two numbers in two adjacent cells.
2 Select both cells.
3 AutoFill down the rows or across the columns.

If you want to enter dates, you can use the Fill option. The date
can be incremented using every day of the week (day), weekdays
only (Monday to Friday), months or years.

1 Enter the first date in your series.
2 Click and drag the Fill Handle using the right mouse button.

3 When you release, a pop-up menu appears.
4 Select the fill option you require – Fill Days, Fill Weekdays, Fill Months or Fill Years.

Examples of some of the Fill options are displayed above.

■ Columns C and D show different day formats AutoFilled.
■ Column E shows figures with an increment of 10 AutoFilled.
■ Column F has been completed using the Fill Years option on the pop-up menu.
■ Column G has been completed using the Fill Months option on the pop-up menu.

	C	D	E	F	G
		Fill Weekdays	Step Value 10	Fill Years	Fill Months
1					
2	Monday	Mon	10	01/01/2010	01/01/2010
3	Tuesday	Tue	20	01/01/2011	01/02/2010
4	Wednesday	Wed	30	01/01/2012	01/03/2010
5	Thursday	Thu	40	01/01/2013	01/04/2010
6	Friday	Fri	50	01/01/2014	01/05/2010
7	Saturday	Mon	60	01/01/2015	01/06/2010
8	Sunday	Tue	70	01/01/2016	01/07/2010
9	Monday	Wed	80	01/01/2017	01/08/2010
10	Tuesday	Thu	90	01/01/2018	01/09/2010
11	Wednesday	Fri	100	01/01/2019	01/10/2010
12	Thursday	Mon	110	01/01/2020	01/11/2010
13	Friday	Tue	120	01/01/2021	01/12/2010

(Spreadsheet: File Home Insert Page Layout Formulas Data Review View — cell G18 — TY Excel 2010 Examples - Microsoft)

2.12 Another worksheet!

Use this example to get some more practice. Enter the text and data below into a different worksheet in your workbook. To select a different worksheet, click the sheet tab – Sheet1, Sheet2, Sheet 3, etc. to the left of the horizontal scroll bar. It doesn't matter what sheet you use. This example is for a stock value table for Screw the Nut plc. Use the following notes to help you get the layout and formulas correct.

- Enter the titles and column headings, Part No, Description, Cost (trade), Cost (retail), Profit, Number in Stock and Value of Stock.
- Format row 5 to allow text wrap in the cells (see section 2.8).
- Format the data cells in the Cost (trade), Cost (retail), Profit and Value of Stock columns to display the figures as currency (see section 2.9).
- Enter a formula to calculate the Profit figure. For the first item (screwdriver set) it would be =D6-C6 (see section 2.10 for information on entering formulas).
- The Number in Stock figures are centred in this example (see section 3.2 for more on alignment).
- Enter a formula to calculate the Value of Stock column. For the first item it would be =C6*F6 (if you base the stock value on the trade price).
- AutoFill the formulas down the columns (see section 2.11).
- The Total value of Stock figure could be calculated by entering the formula =G6+G7+G8+G9 (you could also use the AutoSum function for this – see section 5.1).

	A	B	C	D	E	F	G
1	SCREW THE NUT PLC						
2							
3	Stock Value Data						
4							
5	Part No	Description	Cost (trade)	Cost (retail)	Profit	Number in Stock	Value of Stock
6	S113	Screwdriver Set	£ 10.00	£ 18.99	£ 8.99	4	£ 40.00
7	S2451	Spanner set	£ 14.00	£ 20.99	£ 6.99	6	£ 84.00
8	W2201	Wrench and Grip set	£ 9.00	£ 15.99	£ 6.99	6	£ 54.00
9	W3120	Workman (B&D)	£ 60.00	£ 75.00	£ 15.00	3	£180.00
10							
11						Total value of stock	£ 358.00

2.13 Move or copy cell contents

If you enter text or data into your worksheet, and it's correct, but in the wrong place you can move it to where it should be (rather than delete it and re-type it in the correct location).

To move the contents of cells:

Cut and Paste
1 Select the cells you want to move.
2 Click the **Cut** tool in the **Clipboard** group on the **Home** tab.
3 Select the top leftmost cell of the range you want to move the text or data to.
4 Click the **Paste** tool in the **Clipboard** group.

Cut

Paste

Or

Drag and Drop
1 Select the cells you want to move.
2 Point to the edge of the selected area – the mouse pointer displays four directional arrows.
3 Drag and drop the cells into the new position.

To copy the contents of cells:

Copy and Paste
1 Select the cells you want to copy.
2 Click the **Copy** tool in the **Clipboard** group.
■ A dotted line appears around the cells.
3 Select the top left cell of the range to copy the data to.
4 Click the **Paste** tool in the **Clipboard** group.
■ If you want more than one copy, repeat steps 3 and 4 until you have all the copies required.

Copy

- When you paste, a Smart tag appears below the data. Click this to display the paste options and select one if you do not want the default.

5 Press [Esc] to cancel the dotted line around the copied cells.

Or

Drag and Drop

1 Select the cells you want to copy.

2 Point to the edge of the selected area – the mouse pointer displays four directional arrows.

3 Hold down [Ctrl] (the pointer changes to a white arrow with + beside it) while you drag and drop the cells. Release the mouse button before [Ctrl] – if you don't, you'll move the cells instead of copying them.

Paste Special

Paste Special allows you to be selective about what you paste – the functions, formatting, comments, etc. – or to paste data and add, subtract, multiply or divide it into existing data.

1 Copy or cut the data.

2 Select the cell(s) to paste the data into.

3 Click the arrow beneath the **Paste** button.

4 Select an option from the list.

Or

Click Paste Special...

5 Select what to paste from the dialog box.

6 Choose the operation to perform with the pasted data (if any).

7 Click **OK**.

Author's insight

If you want to move or copy some cells, and insert them between existing rows of columns:

1 Select the cells you want to move or copy.
2 Drag and drop using the *right* mouse button.
3 At the shortcut menu choose the option required, e.g. Shift Down and Copy; Shift Right and Move; etc.

2.14 Insert/delete rows and columns

As you build up your worksheet, you may discover that you have added a row or column that you don't require, or have perhaps missed out a row or column that you do need.

To insert a row:
1 Select the row (see section 2.4) that will go below the row you are inserting.
2 Right-click within the selected area and choose **Insert** from the pop-up menu.

To insert a column:

  1 Select the column (see section 2.4) that will go to the right of the column you are inserting.

  2 Right-click within the selected area and choose **Insert**.

To delete a row or column:

  1 Select the row or column (see section 2.4) you wish to delete.

  2 Right-click within the selected area and choose **Delete**.

To add or delete several rows or columns at the same time:

  1 Click and drag in the row or column label area to indicate how many rows or columns you want to insert or delete.

  2 Right-click in the selected area and choose **Insert** or **Delete**.

2.15 View options

The way your worksheet appears on the screen is influenced by the view options you have selected. There are many options that can change the way your worksheet looks. We will consider some of the more commonly used ones here – others will be introduced as appropriate throughout the book.

ZOOM

The Zoom affects the size of your worksheet on the screen. The default zoom is 100%, but you can increase this to make your worksheet easier to read, or decrease it so you can see more information on the screen at one time.

To change the zoom option:

  ■ Click the increase (plus) and decrease (minus) buttons at the bottom right of the status bar.

Or

  ■ Click and drag the slider on the Zoom control.

NORMAL, PAGE LAYOUT AND PAGE BREAK VIEWS

Most people work in Normal view when developing their worksheets. Other regularly-used views are:

▶ **Page Layout** – *which shows the margin area and header and footer areas of a page as well as the print area.*
▶ **Page Break Preview** – *which shows you where the page breaks will be if you print your worksheet.*

There are tools for each of these views to the left of the zoom area on the Status bar.

Normal   Decrease Zoom   Increase Zoom

Page Layout

Page Break Preview

View tab

You will also find view options on the **View** tab in the Ribbon. The **Workbook View** group contains **Normal, Page Layout** and **Page Break Preview** command buttons and the **Zoom** group has additional zoom options.

2.16 Print

At some stage you will want to print your file. Before printing, you may have to adjust some of the Page Layout options to get a good fit. Page layout options are discussed in section 3.9.

PRINT

■ Click the **File** tab, and select **Print**.

A preview of the current worksheet will be displayed on the right of your screen, in Full Page view. It doesn't matter if you can't read what is on the screen – the preview is there to let you see how your worksheet will fit onto your paper. You get an idea of how well the data, white space, graphics, etc. will look on the page.

To change something when you see the preview:
1 Click the **Home** tab (or other tab) to return to your worksheet.
2 Edit the worksheet as required.
3 Choose **Print** again to see how it looks.

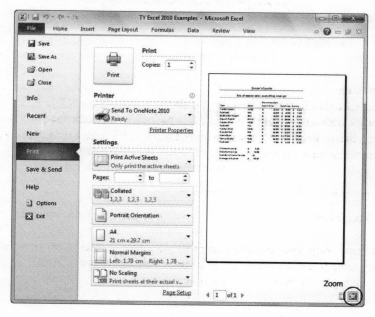

When you are happy with the preview, you can send it to print.

1 Specify the number of copies required.
2 Click **Print**.

To select print options:
1 Click the Microsoft Office button and select **Print**.
2 Specify the options in the **Print** dialog box and click **OK**.

To print part of your worksheet:

If you don't want to print all of your worksheet, you can print the area required on its own.

1 Select the range of cells you want to print.
2 Choose **Print** in Backstage view.
3 Under **Settings**, choose **Print Selection**.
4 **Print**.

THINGS TO REMEMBER

1   *The worksheet is a grid of cells, identified by their column letters and row numbers.*

2   *A block of cells is called a range. Cells and ranges can be given names to use instead of their column/row addresses.*

3   *The main file handling commands are Save, Close, Open and New.*

4   *You can move around a worksheet by scrolling and clicking into cells with the mouse, or by using the arrow keys.*

5   *You can select rows, columns, adjacent and non-adjacent cells using the mouse of the keyboard.*

6   *A cell may contain text, numbers or a formula. You can delete, replace or edit the contents of a cell.*

7   *Column widths can be adjusted, and you can wrap text within a cell and 'shrink to fit'.*

8   *Numbers can be formatted in different ways.*

9   *When writing a formula, follow the BODMAS rules.*

10 *AutoFill can copy formulas or produce data series.*

11 *You can insert and delete rows and columns if necessary.*

TEST

1 *The grid of an Excel worksheet consists of:*
   a *Workbooks, worksheets and tabs*
   b *Rows, columns and cells*
   c *Formulas, functions and text*
   d *Ribbons, groups and buttons*

2 *A cell can contain:*
   a *Text*
   b *Data*
   c *Formula*
   d *Function*
   e *All of the above*

3 *What do the following keyboard shortcuts do?*
   a *[Ctrl]-[N]*
   b *[F12]*
   c *[Ctrl]-[O]*
   d *[Ctrl]-[S]*

4 *Suggest two ways of displaying the GoTo dialog box.*

5 *How do you select non-adjacent cells?*

6 *What does ######## in a cell indicate?*

7 *Suggest three cell formatting options.*

8 *Identify three number formats.*

9 *What formula is in cell D2?*

	A	B	C	D
1	**Employee**	**Basic pay**	**Overtime**	**Gross pay**
2	AB1023	£ 265.00	£ 57.60	£ 322.60

   a *=A2+B2*
   b *=B2+C2*
   c *B2+C2*
   d *=B2-C2*

10 *Page Layout view displays:*
   a *Formulas and functions*
   b *Print area and header and footer areas*
   c *Only where page breaks occur*
   d *Printing options.*

Formatting and layout

In this chapter you will learn:
- *some more formatting options*
- *how to freeze panes*
- *how to split the screen*
- *how to set page layout options*

3.1 Font group

The most commonly used Font formatting options are located in the Font group on the Home tab.

Some of the buttons are toggles, e.g. Bold, Italic and Underline – click to select or deselect the format. Others, e.g. Font, Font Size, Border, Cell Fill Colour and Font Colour – have drop-down arrows that display their options

- To access the **Font** tab in the **Format Cells** dialog box, click the **Format Cells** dialog box launcher button at the bottom right corner of the **Font** group. This tab has a few more formatting options than are found in the **Font** group.

BOLD, ITALIC AND UNDERLINE

To apply/remove bold, italic or single underline formatting:
1 Select the cell(s) you wish to format.
2 Click **B** or **I** or **U** to apply or remove the format.
3 Deselect the cell(s).

To apply double underline, click the drop-down arrow to the right of the underline button, and select **Double Underline**.

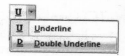

FONT AND FONT SIZE

The default font used in Excel is Calibri, the default font size is 11. You can use the **Font** or **Font Size** command button to change these settings if you wish.

To change the font or font size:
1 Select the cell(s) you wish to change the formatting for.
2 Click the arrow to the right of the **Font** or **Font Size** button.
3 Select the font or size – if you hover over an option you will get a live preview of that option in the selected cell(s)
4 Deselect the cell(s).

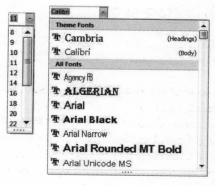

■ The Increase **Font Size** and **Decrease Font Size** buttons [A+] [A-] can be used to change the font size. Select the cell(s), then click the **Increase** or **Decrease Font Size** button to set the size.

■ You can type the name or size into the Font or Font Size field and press [**Enter**] to change the font or size.

Default Font

The default font is the one that is used each time you create a new workbook (Calibri, 11 initially). If you nearly always change this font to a different font for your workbook, it would be quicker and easier in the long run if you change the default font.

To change the default font:

1 Click **File** to go into Backstage view and choose **Options**.
2 Select **General** from the list of options on the left.
3 Specify the font you wish to use in the **Use this font:** field.
4 Set the default font size in the **Font size** field.
5 Click **OK**.

■ You will need to restart Excel for your settings to take effect. All new workbooks will be affected by this change – existing workbooks will not be affected.

FONT COLOUR

To change the colour of the font:
1 Select the cell(s).
2 Click the arrow to the right of the
   Font Color button.
■ The font colour of the selected cell(s)
   changes automatically as you move
   the pointer over the colours.
3 Select the colour required.
■ Click **More Colors...** to access the
   Color dialog box and even more
   colours.
4 Deselect the cell(s).

■ If you display a list of options, e.g. the font or colour, and
   then decide that you do not want to choose anything, just click
   anywhere on your worksheet to cancel the procedure.

FILL COLOUR

To change the fill colour of your cell(s):
1 Select the cell(s).
2 Click the arrow to the right of the **Fill
   Color** button.
3 Select the colour required.
4 Deselect your cell(s).
■ You will find more fill options, e.g. fill
   effects and pattern options, on the **Fill**
   tab in the **Format Cells** dialog box.

Author's insight

There are a huge range of fill colours and effects in Excel
(and throughout the Office suite).

Too much manual formatting of cells can result in a poorly
formatted worksheet – unless you have a particular flair for
this sort of thing.

(Contd)

A more professional look can often be achieved by using a Theme, and customizing it to suit.

Themes are discussed in Chapter 4.

BORDERS

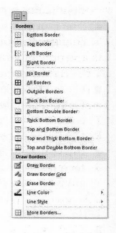

To apply borders to your cells:
1 Select the cell(s).
2 Click the arrow to the right of the **Border** button.
3 Select the border option required.
Or
4 Click **More Borders...** to display the **Borders** tab of the **Format Cells** dialog box for more options.

LIVE PREVIEW

Live Preview results in selected cells being automatically formatted – albeit as a preview – when you move the mouse over the different formatting options. It can be a really useful feature as it reduces the format, undo, format cycle as you experiment with different formatting options. When you find the formatting you want, you can then apply it and move on. If someone has switched the feature off, or if you really don't like it (and I would recommend you try it for a while before you decide) you will find the option to switch it on/off in the Excel Options dialog box.

1 Click the **File** tab and choose **Options**.
2 In the **General** options, select or deselect **Enable Live Preview** as required.
3 Click **OK**.

3.2 Alignment group

When you enter data into your cells, the default horizontal alignment is left for text, and right for numbers. The default vertical alignment or text and numbers is at the bottom.

The Alignment group on the Home tab has a variety of alignment options to choose from.

To align data horizontally within a cell:
1 Select the cell(s) you wish to format.
2 Click the **Align Left, Center** or **Align Right** button in the top row.
3 Deselect the cell(s).

To align a cell entry with the top, middle or bottom of a cell:
1 Select the cell(s) you wish to format.
2 Click the **Top, Middle** or **Bottom Align** button in the bottom row.
3 Deselect the cell(s).

To change the orientation of a cell entry:
The orientation of a cell entry is often adjusted when labelling narrow columns.

1 Select the cell(s).
2 Click the arrow beside the **Orientation** button.
3 Select the option required.
4 Deselect the cell(s).

Some of the alignment options are displayed here:

Left align	Center align	Right align	
Top align			V e r t i c a l t e x t
	Middle align		
		Bottom align	
	Rotate text up	Rotate text down	
Counterclockwise		Clockwise	

WRAP TEXT

If you want text to display in one cell, rather than adjust the width if the text doesn't fit, you can wrap it within the cell. The row height will then adjust to accommodate the entry.

1 Select the cell(s) you wish to format.
2 Click the **Wrap text** command button.
3 Deselect the cell(s).

MERGE CELLS

Worksheet headings (rather than column headings) often run across several columns. You can easily merge the cells in the heading row to improve the layout of your worksheet.

■ Ensure that the text you wish displayed in the merged cell is in the top left-most cell of those to be merged. Any data not in the top left-most cell is lost as a result of the merge.

MERGE AND CENTER

1   Select the cells you wish to merge.
2   Click the **Merge and Center** button.

To merge cells without centring the data:

1   Select the cells you wish to merge.
2   Click the arrow to the right of the
    Merge and Center button.
3   Select **Merge Across** from the options.
■   You could also use the **Merge Cells**
    option for this.

To UnMerge cells:
1   Select the cell.
2   Click the arrow to the right of the **Merge and Center** button.
3   Select **UnMerge Cells**.

INDENT

To change the space between the text and the left of the cell:

1   Select the cell(s).
2   Click the **Increase Indent** or **Decrease Indent** button until you
    have the effect you want.
■   To access the **Alignment** tab in
    the **Format Cells** dialog box,
    click the **Alignment** dialog box
    launcher button at the bottom
    right of the **Alignment** group.

Alignment dialog box launcher

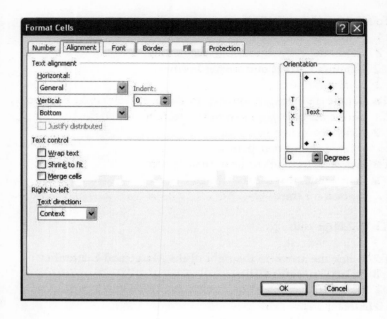

3.3 Number formats

Many of the cells in a worksheet will contain numeric data – monetary figures, percentages, integers, etc. The most commonly used number formats are in the Number group on the Home tab.

The Category field shows the category of the selected cell.

To change the category:
■ Click the drop-down arrow and select the category from the list.

To format cells as currency – £:
1 Select the cell(s).
2 Click the **Accounting Number Format** button in the **Number** group.

To format cells as currency – euro or dollar:
1 Select the cell(s).
2 Click the arrow beside the **Accounting Number Format** button 🔳 ▾.
3 Select an option.
■ To use a different currency, click **More Accounting Formats...** and select the options from the **Number** tab in the **Format Cells** dialog box.

To format using the Percent style or Comma style:
1 Select the cell(s).
2 Click the **Percent Style** 🔳 or **Comma Style** 🔳 button in the **Number** group.
3 Deselect your cell(s).

To change the number of decimal places displayed in a figure:
1 Select the cell(s).
2 Click the **Increase** 🔳 or **Decrease Decimal** 🔳 button.
3 Deselect your cell(s).

Additional number formatting options can be found on the **Number** tab in the **Format Cells** dialog box – click the **Format Cells** dialog box launcher button at the bottom right of the **Number** group.

Author's insight

There is an extensive range of number formats to suit virtually any situation. Currency and Accounting are perhaps the most commonly used, along with Comma and Percent styles.

The Number Format list in the Number group gives quick access to commonly used date, time, fraction and text formats (useful when entering numbers into a cell where you want them to be treated like text, e.g. a numeric product code).

The Number tab in the Format Cells dialog box will give you access to the whole range.

3.4 Format Painter

If you have applied several formatting options to a cell, and you want to apply the same formatting to some other cells in your worksheet you could save yourself some time by using the Format Painter.

The Format Painter allows you to copy the formatting from one cell, and paint it on to other cells.

To copy a format to a single cell, or to adjacent cells:
1 Select the cell that is formatted the way you want.
2 Click the **Format Painter** button in the **Clipboard** group on the **Home** tab.
3 Click on the cell to apply the formatting.

Or
■ Click and drag over the cells to apply the formatting.

To copy a format to non-adjacent cells:
1 Select the cell that is formatted the way you want.
2 Double-click the **Format Painter** button – this 'locks' the Format Painter tool on.
3 Click on each cell to apply the formatting.

Or
1 Drag over the cells you want to paint with the formatting.
2 Click the **Format Painter** button again (or press [**Esc**]) to switch the Format Painter off when you've finished.

Keyboard shortcuts
Useful keyboard shortcuts when formatting cells:

■ [Ctrl]-[B] or [Ctrl]-[2]	toggles bold
■ [Ctrl]-[I] or [Ctrl]-[3]	toggles italics
■ [Ctrl]-[U] or [Ctrl]-[4]	toggles underline
■ [Ctrl]-[5]	toggles strikethrough

■ [Ctrl]-[Z]	Undo
■ [Ctrl]-[Spacebar]	selects an entire column in a worksheet
■ [Shift]-[Spacebar]	selects an entire row in a worksheet
■ [Ctrl]-[A]	selects whole workbook

3.5 Standard styles

A style is a set of formatting options that you save as a group. When you want to apply the formats held in a style, you apply the style, rather than each of the formatting options individually.

If you don't apply a style to text or data, it is formatted using the Normal style.

If you format data using the Accounting Number Format, Comma Style or Percent Style buttons in the Number group you are applying a predefined style. Other predefined styles in the Cell Styles list are: Currency (zero decimal places) and Comma (zero decimal places).

Using styles has two main benefits:
▶ *Consistency – when you apply a style, all the formatting options contained within it are applied in one go (you won't accidentally use the wrong font size or colour).*
▶ *Speed – it's usually quicker to apply a style than to apply several options individually using the command buttons.*

You can apply a style to an individual cell, or a group of cells.
1 Select the cell(s) you wish to apply a style to.
2 Click **Cell Styles** in the **Cells** group on the **Home** tab.
3 Select the style required.

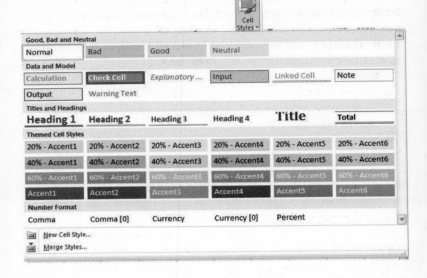

- Note that the Cell Styles also has Number formats.

Apply some styles to your Simon's Sports worksheet. Use the Titles and Headings styles, or the Themed Cell Styles, e.g.:

- Heading 1 to the 'Simon's Sports' heading,
- Heading 2 to the 'End of Season Sale – Everything must go!!'
- Heading 3 to the column headings in the Simon's Sports worksheet.

We will discuss creating your own styles in Chapter 8.

3.6 Conditional formatting

Conditional formatting is used to format a cell (or range of cells), if specific conditions are met. It's useful if you want to be able to highlight cells that contain values that are higher or lower than you would expect, or within a certain range. By applying conditional formatting you can identify such data at a glance. For example, you may have a list of figures, and want all those that are >=50000 (more than or equal to) displayed in red and italics, and all those figures that are <50000 (less than) in green.

> ▶ *When creating a conditional format you can reference other cells in the same worksheet, e.g. = FA5000, but you cannot use references to an external workbook.*

To apply a conditional format:

1 Select the cells that you want to apply the formatting to.

2 Click the **Conditional Formatting** button in the **Styles** group on the **Home** tab.

3 Select **Highlight Cells Rules**.

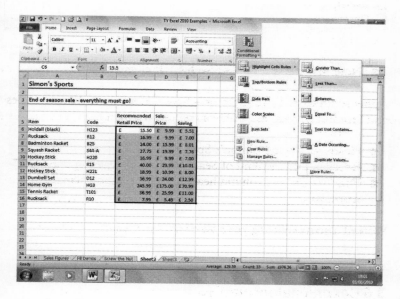

4 Select the rule.

5 Complete the dialog box with details of your new rule.

6 Click **OK**.

7 Repeat steps 1–6 for each rule you want applied to the cells.

If you wish to create a new rule for highlighting cells, select the **More Rules...** option at the bottom of the **Highlight Cells Rules** list, and complete the dialog box with details of the rule you wish to set up.

To clear rules:

1 Select the cells that have rules applied (if necessary).
2 Click the **Conditional Formatting** button.
3 Select **Clear Rules**.
4 Click on **Selected Cells** or **Entire Sheet**, depending on where you wish to remove the rules from.

TOP/BOTTOM RULES

This allows you to quickly format the specified top or bottom:
- number of items
- percentage of items, or
- those above or below average.

DATA BARS, COLOR SCALES AND ICON SETS

You can quickly add a Data Bar, Color Scale or Icon Set formatting option to a range of scales using the preset formats available, or by customizing these to suit your requirements.

1 Select the cells to format.
2 Click the **Conditional Formatting** button.
3 Select **Data Bars** or **Color Scales** or **Icon Sets**.
4 Choose the one you wish to use.
- To customize any of the settings, or set up another rule, click **More Rules...** and complete the dialog box as required.

FORMAT AS TABLE

The Format as Table Gallery displays predefined fill and border formats that you can apply to the cells in your worksheet.

The limit of what is formatted is determined either by:

▶ *A blank row and/or column to indicate the end of the data area*

Or

▶ *The range of cells that you have selected*

To apply a Format as Table format:

1 Identify the area to be formatted.

2 Select the format required from the **Format as Table** gallery.

3 At the dialog box, select or deselect the checkbox to indicate depending on whether or not the range has a header row (a row containing column headings).

4 Click **OK**.

Format as Table also adds a Filter to the header row in your cell range.

See Chapter 9 for details on filtering data.

There are various ways of removing the formatting/filter from your table. On the **Table Design** tab you could:

■ Choose **Clear** from the bottom of the **Format as Table** gallery.
Or
■ Click **Convert to Range** in the **Tools** group.

3.7 Freeze panes

Many of the worksheets you create will be considerably larger than will fit on to your computer screen. You will need to scroll vertically and horizontally to display the data you want to work with. When you scroll your worksheet, the column headings or row labels will disappear off your screen as the other data appears. This is often inconvenient, as you need to see the headings and labels to make sense of your data. In these situations you should freeze the heading columns and rows so that they stay in place and only the data cells scroll.

To freeze the top row or the first column:

1 Select the **View** tab on the Ribbon.

2 Click the **Freeze Panes** button in the **Window** group.

3 Select **Freeze Top Row** or **Freeze First Column**.

To freeze a row (or rows):

1 Select the row below the ones you want to freeze.

Or

To freeze a column (or columns):

■ Select the column to the right of the ones you want to freeze.

Or

To freeze both a row (or rows) and column (or columns):

■ Select the cell below and to the right of where you want to freeze the panes.

2 Open the Window menu.

3 Choose **Freeze Panes**.

The worksheet will be divided into separate panes.

When you scroll through your worksheet horizontally, the column or columns you have frozen remain in view. When you scroll through your worksheet vertically the row or rows you have frozen will remain in view when the other data scrolls.

The heavy line indicates the edge of the frozen pane
Rows 1–5 are frozen

	A	B	C	D	E
1	**Simon's Sports**				
2					
3	**End of season sale - everything must go!**				
4					
5	Item	Code	Recommended Retail Price	Sale Price	Saving
12	Hockey Stick	H221	£ 18.99	£ 10.99	£ 8.00
13	Dumbell Set	D12	£ 36.99	£ 24.00	£ 12.99
14	Home Gym	HG3	£ 245.99	£ 175.00	£ 70.99
15	Tennis Racket	T101	£ 36.99	£ 25.99	£ 11.00
16	Rucksack	R10	£ 7.99	£ 5.49	£ 2.50

To unfreeze panes:

1 Click the **Freeze Panes** command button.
2 Choose **Unfreeze Panes**.

3.8 Split screen

There will also be times when you want to compare the data on
one part of your worksheet with that on another – but the data
ranges that you want to compare are in separate areas of the
worksheet. When this happens, you should split your screen so
that you can scroll each part independently, to bring the data
you require into view.

When you split the screen, the split will appear above the current
cell, or to the left of the current cell – or both – depending on
where the selected cell is.

1 To split the screen horizontally only, select a cell in column A

Or

- To split the screen vertically only, select a cell in row 1

Or

- To split the screen horizontally and vertically, select the cell that will be below and to the right of the splits.

2 Click the **Split** command in the **Window** group on the **View** tab.

SPLIT BOX

If you look carefully above the top of the vertical scroll bar or just to the right of the horizontal scroll bar, you will notice the split boxes. You can also use these to split your screen.

To split your screen horizontally:

- Drag the split box at the top of the vertical scroll bar down to where you want your split to be (or double-click on it and then drag the split to adjust its position if necessary).

To split your screen vertically:

- Drag the split box at the right of the horizontal scroll bar along to where you want your split to be (or double-click on it and then drag the split to adjust its position if necessary).

When your screen is split, you can scroll each pane independently to view the data you want to see.

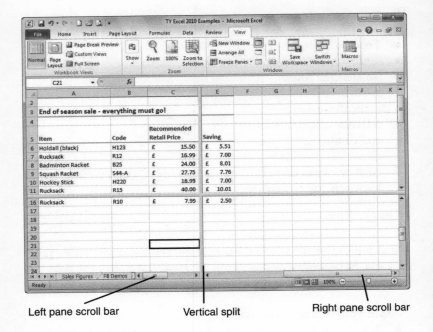

Left pane scroll bar   Vertical split   Right pane scroll bar

To remove a split:
■ Double-click on it.

3.9 Page setup

In Chapter 2 we discussed printing. We will now consider some ways in which you can change the appearance (or layout) of the printed sheet.

MARGINS

The margin is the amount of white space between the edge of the paper and where your worksheet area starts.

The normal margin settings are:

- ► *Top and bottom – 1.91 cm*
- ► *Right and left – 1.78 cm*
- ► *Header and footer – 0.76 cm.*

To change these margins:

1 Select the **Page Layout** tab on the Ribbon.
2 Click the **Margins** button in the **Page Setup** group.
3 Choose **Wide** or **Narrow** margins.

Or

4 Click **Custom Margins...** to display the dialog box, where you can specify the exact measurements you require.

ORIENTATION

Pages are usually printed portrait (rather than landscape), and on A4 paper.

To change the orientation:

1 Select the **Page Layout** tab.
2 Click the **Orientation** button in the **Page Setup** group.
3 Choose the orientation.

PAPER SIZE

The default paper size is A4.

1 Click the **Size** button in the **Page Setup** group on the **Page Layout** tab.
2 Select the paper size required from the list.

Or

3 Click **More Paper Sizes...** and select the size from the dialog box.

PRINT AREA

If you regularly print part of your worksheet, you can specify the range as a print area. This is the area that Excel will then print as the default. A print area remains set until you clear it.

To set the print area:
1 Select the range of cells.
2 Go to the **Page Setup** group on the **Page Layout** tab.
3 Click **Print Area**.
4 Select **Set Print Area**.
■ If you have a print area set, and wish to print a different range you can do so using print selection (see below).

If you have a print area set and wish to print the whole worksheet:

1 Click the **File** tab to display Backstage view.
2 Select **Print**.
3 Under **Settings**, drop down the list of options.
4 Select the **Ignore print area** checkbox.

To remove a print area:
1 Go to the **Page Setup** group on the **Page Layout** tab.
2 Click **Print Area**.
3 Select **Clear Print Area**.
■ If you have a print area set, you can select additional cells and add them to the print area. These will normally be adjacent to those in the original print area.

PRINT SELECTION

You can print any part of your worksheet, whether a print area is set or not.

1 Select the range of cells you wish to print.
2 Click the **File** tab to display Backstage view.
3 Select **Print**.
4 Under **Settings**, drop down the list of options.
5 Select **Print Selection**.

BREAKS

Page breaks are inserted automatically by Excel if your data will not fit onto one sheet of paper. If the automatic page breaks do not occur exactly where you would want them, you can insert manual page breaks.

1 To insert a horizontal page break, select the row (or select the cell in column A) below which you want it.

Or

■ To insert a vertical page break, select the column (or select the cell in row 1) to the right of which you want it.

Or

■ To insert a horizontal and vertical page break at the same time, select the cell immediately below and to the right of where you want to start a new page.

2 Click the **Breaks** button on the **Page Setup** group.

3 Select **Insert Page Break**. A page break will be inserted above the current row or to the left of the current column.

To remove a page break:

1 Select any cell in the row below the page break you wish to remove.

Or

■ Select any cell in the column to the right of the page break you wish to remove.

2 Click the **Breaks** button on the **Page Setup** group.

3 Select **Remove Page Break**.

To remove all page breaks:

1 Select any cell in your worksheet.

2 Click the **Breaks** button on the **Page Setup** group.

3 Select **Reset All Page Breaks**.

BACKGROUND

The Background option lets you display an image on the background of your worksheet. This can improve the appearance of the screen or of a web page, but note that these do not print.

1 Select any cell in the worksheet.
2 Click the **Background** button on the **Page Setup** group.
3 Browse through your folders until you find the image you wish to use.
4 Select the image.
5 Click **Insert**.
■ To remove a background, click the **Delete Background** button (the **Background** button changes to this when a background is applied).
■ Depending on the background selected, you may find it difficult to read your data with this formatting applied. You could try hiding the gridlines, or applying a fill colour to cells with data to improve readability.

PRINT TITLES

If you are printing a worksheet with a list of data that runs over several pages, you might find the printout easier to read if you have the column and/or row titles repeated on each page.

1 Click **Print Titles** in the **Page Setup** group.
2 On the **Sheet** tab, specify the rows and/or columns that you want to repeat on each page.
■ Click and drag on the row numbers or column letters (move the dialog box if necessary, so you can see them) or type them, e.g. $1:$4 for rows 1–4, or $A:$B for columns A and B.
3 Click **OK**.

Page Setup dialog box

Many of the options discussed in this section can be found on the various tabs in the Page Setup dialog box.

You can access this dialog box from several places by clicking the dialog box launcher button that is in most of the groups on the Page Layout tab.

SCALE TO FIT

If a worksheet is more than a page in size, you can specify the number of pages you want it to be printed on using the Scale to Fit group on the Page Layout tab.

■ Specify the number of pages wide in the Width field and/or the number of pages high in the Height field.

Or

- Leave both the Width and Height field at automatic, and set the percentage scaling that you wish to use.

Scaling can be very useful if the last page of your worksheet contains only a small amount of data. You can specify that the worksheet prints on one page less than it really needs – Excel will scale it down to fit onto that number of pages.

PAGE ORDER

If your worksheet is going to print out on more than one sheet of paper, the pages can be printed down then over or over then down. You can specify the order you prefer.

1 Open the **Page Setup** dialog box – if you do so from the **Sheet Options** group, it will take you straight to the **Sheet** tab in the dialog box.
2 On the **Sheet** tab, select the **Page Order** option required.
3 Click **OK**.

GRIDLINES, ROW AND COLUMN HEADINGS

When you print your worksheet out, the gridlines, row and column headings do not normally print. This is usually how you would want it, but there may be times when it is useful to print out the gridlines and/or the headings – for example, when printing out the formulas and functions (see Chapter 5).

To print the gridlines:
- Tick the **Print** checkbox in the **Gridlines** section of the **Sheet Options** group.

To print the row and column headings:
- Tick the **Print** option in the **Headings** section of the **Sheet Options** group.

Gridlines and borders

It is important that you differentiate between gridlines and borders.

Gridlines are displayed around the cell boundaries on your screen – to help you identify the columns and rows and read your worksheet data.

The gridlines can be switched on and off from the View tab, Show/Hide group.

Gridlines do not normally print – if you do a Print Preview when your gridlines are displayed they will not appear in the preview (and they won't print).

If you want your gridlines to print, you must switch this option on (Page Layout tab, Sheet group, Gridlines, Print).

Gridlines will surround *every* cell – you cannot switch them on and off for part of the worksheet.

Borders – to identify key areas in your worksheet, surround totals or enhance the readability of your worksheet – are usually printed.

Borders can be placed around cell ranges, or above and below cell ranges, etc. to create the effect you want.

HEADERS AND FOOTERS

Headers and footers display information at the top or bottom of every page that prints out for your worksheet. They are useful for page numbers, your name, the date that the worksheet is printed, the worksheet name, the workbook name – or any other information that you would like to appear in them.

To add a header and/or footer to your pages:

1   Go to the **Insert** tab.
2   Click the **Header & Footer** button in the **Text** group.

3 The insertion point moves to the centre of the header, and the **Header & Footer** tools are displayed on the **Design** tab.

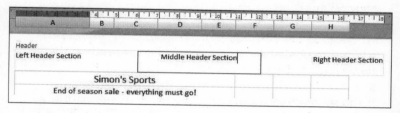

4 There are three sections to the header and footer area – left, middle and right. To move from one to another, click in it, or press [**Tab**] to cycle through the sections.

5 Type your header and/or footer in through the keyboard.

Or

6 To insert a standard header or footer, with combinations of the sheet name, workbook name and other elements, select one from the Header and Footer lists.

Or

7 To insert individual standard elements, click the appropriate button in the **Header & Footer** elements group.

To move between the Header and Footer area:

■ Use the buttons in the **Navigation** group.

Other options are available in the **Options** group.

When you choose the Header & Footer command, Excel takes
your worksheet into Page Layout view.

To return to Normal view:
   1 Click within the worksheet area.
   2 Choose **Normal** view.

Author's insight

Headers and footers can also be added from Page Layout
view.

■ Click the Page Layout view icon on the Status bar.
Or
■ Display the **View** tab, and select **Page Layout** from the
   Workbook views group.

THINGS TO REMEMBER

1 *You can format the font and alignment of cell contents, and the display of numbers.*

2 *You can copy formatting from one cell to others using the Format Painter.*

3 *Styles can simplify formatting.*

4 *Conditional formatting changes to suit the contents of cells.*

5 *You can freeze panes or split the screen to bring distant parts of the worksheet into view at the same time.*

6 *The page layout options allow you to set the margins, orientation, headers and footers and other aspects.*

TEST

1   What is the difference between a FILL colour and a FONT colour?

2   What are the potential benefits of using cell styles rather than manual formatting?

3   You would like to format all the cells containing numbers >=60 with a Green Fill and Dark Green Text. What feature should you use?

4   When would you use the Freeze panes feature?

5   Where would you find the Split Box(es).

6   You have set a print area. If you preview your worksheet, without specifying any other options, Excel will display the:
    a   Whole worksheet
    b   Whole workbook
    c   Print area

7   Horizontal and vertical page breaks can be inserted where required – true or false?

8   An image added to the worksheet background will print in full colour only – true or false.

9   Explain the differences between gridlines and borders.

10 You want your name, the current date and the page number displayed on every page when your worksheet is printed. Where should you add this information?

4

Working with sheets

In this chapter you will learn:

- *about worksheet layout*
- *how to insert, delete and rename worksheets*
- *about moving and copying worksheets*
- *how to group worksheets*
- *to change the tab colour*

4.1 Moving between worksheets

The worksheet tabs appear at the bottom left of your screen – to the left of the horizontal scrollbar.

To move from one sheet to another in your workbook:

- Click the sheet tab of the sheet you want to work on.

If you can't see all the sheet tabs in the sheet tab bar, you can use the buttons to the left of the sheet tabs to scroll the sheet tabs into view.

You can change the amount of space allocated to the sheet tab bar and the horizontal scroll bar by dragging the tab split box between the sheet tabs and the horizontal scroll bar.

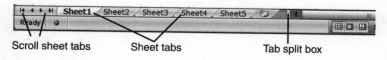

Scroll sheet tabs   Sheet tabs   Tab split box

4.2 Worksheet design

Before you start setting up a worksheet, you should give some thought to its design.

- ▶ *Work out the purpose of your worksheet. Ask yourself:*
  - ▷ *What do you want to communicate?*
  - ▷ *What should be emphasized or de-emphasized?*
  - ▷ *How will you show the relationship between areas?*
- ▶ *Keep it simple.*
- ▶ *Be consistent – within a worksheet and across worksheets. If you produce the same worksheet every month, regular readers will be able to find the information they need quickly if it's always in the same place.*
- ▶ *Use formatting and layout options to add contrast to different areas of your worksheet.*

There are no hard and fast rules – the main objective is to display the data in a clear and unambiguous way. If you like your worksheet layout and your audience can understand it, it's probably okay.

Some Dos and Don'ts of worksheet design

DO make sure you use a font that is easy to read – Calibri (the default) is a very 'clean' font, Times New Roman is easy on the eye when reading from hard copy.

DO use 'white space' – leave some blank rows or columns between sections of your worksheet to make it easier to read.

DO use borders and/or shading effects to divide large worksheets up into manageable chunks and to draw attention to subtotals and totals.

DO format your numbers appropriately – currency, number of decimal places, percentage, etc.

DO make sure your worksheet is legible – don't use too small a font or shrink to fit data to the extent it is too small to read.

DO add comments to cells that need an explanation (see section 5.9).

DON'T use too many different fonts or sizes on a worksheet.

DON'T overdo font and fill colours – you'll give readers a headache!

DON'T print gridlines on a final report – they will give it a very cluttered look, though they may be useful on a draft printout, or one with formulas displayed.

4.3 Themes

You can use themes to quickly and easily apply a set of predefined formats to worksheets and charts. The colours, fonts and effects contained in a theme have been carefully coordinated to give a professional look to your worksheets. A theme is a set of formatting options that includes a colour theme (a set of colours), a font theme (for headings and body text) and an effects theme (for lines and fill effects).

To change the theme:
1 Click **Themes** in the **Themes** group on the **Page Layout** tab.
2 Select the theme that you want.

Initially, you will only see built-in themes to choose from. You may eventually create your own themes – if you do this you will also have the choice of custom themes.

When you change a theme, you will notice that the formatting options on your worksheet change to reflect the settings in the theme you select.

If you applied standard styles in Chapter 3, you will notice that the formatting options in the styles change when you choose a different theme.

You can customize the individual elements of a theme – the colour, font or effect. Select from the options in each group.

CUSTOM THEMES

If you have company colours and formatting specifications to follow you should create a custom theme. On the **Page Layout** tab, **Themes** group:

1 Select a theme to start from – possible the standard Office Theme.
2 Adjust the **Colors** as required – **Save** the colour scheme.

3 Adjust the **Fonts** as required – save the font set.
4 Select the **Effects** option required.
5 At the bottom of the **Themes** drop-down list, choose **Save Current Theme...** and give it a name.

Your Theme will be available for use in Word and PowerPoint too.

4.4 Inserting worksheets

When you create a workbook in Excel the default number of worksheets is three. This may be (more than) enough, but if you need more than three you can easily add them.

To insert a worksheet:
■ Click the **New Worksheet** button to the right of the sheet tabs. A sheet will be added to the end of the workbook.

New worksheet

DEFAULT SHEETS IN A WORKBOOK

If you regularly need to add (or remove) worksheets to get the right number of worksheets in your workbook, you could change the default number of worksheets to a number that is more appropriate for you.

To change the default number of sheets:
1 Click **File** to go to Backstage view and choose.
2 Go to the **General** options.
3 Specify the default number of sheets required.
4 Click **OK**.

Default number of sheets

4.5 Deleting worksheets

If a workbook has too many sheets you can delete any you don't need.

To delete a worksheet:

1 Right-click on the sheet tab of the sheet you want to delete.
2 Select **Delete** from the shortcut menu.
■ If the sheet contains data, you will be asked to confirm the deletion.
3 Respond to the prompt – click **Delete** if you really want to delete the sheet, **Cancel** if you change your mind.

Be careful when deleting sheets – Undo will not restore them!

4.6 Renaming worksheets

By default, worksheets are named Sheet1, Sheet2, etc. If you only use one or two sheets in a workbook this may cause you no problems. If you have several worksheets, life will be easier if you give them a name that actually means something.

To rename a worksheet:
1 Double-click on the sheet tab you want to rename.
2 Type in the name you want to use.
3 Press [**Enter**] or click anywhere on the worksheet.

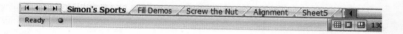

4.7 Moving and copying worksheets

To move or copy a worksheet within a workbook
To move a worksheet using drag and drop:
- Click and drag the worksheet tab of the sheet that you want to move along the sheet tabs until it is in the correct place.

To copy a worksheet using drag and drop:
- Click on a worksheet tab, hold down [Ctrl] and drag it to the required position. The name will have '(2)' after it, to show that the new sheet is a copy. Rename it as required.

To move or copy a worksheet using the dialog box:
1 Right-click on the sheet tab of the one you want to move/copy.
2 Click **Move or Copy...** The Workbook name will be in the To book: field.

3 Select the sheet to move it before – or select (move to end).

4 Select **Create a copy** if a copy is required.

5 Click **OK**.

To move or copy between workbooks

You can easily move or copy a worksheet to another workbook or to a new workbook altogether using the dialog box. If you are moving or copying a worksheet to a different workbook, open the workbook you want to copy/move the sheet to before you start.

1 Right-click on the tab of the sheet to move or copy.

2 Choose **Move** or **Copy** from the shortcut menu.

3 At the dialog box select the workbook you wish to move or copy to in the To book: field.

4 Specify where in the workbook you want the worksheet moved or copied to.

5 Select the checkbox if you want to copy rather than move.

6 Click **OK**.

4.8 Grouping worksheets

There may be times when you want to enter the same text, data or formulas into corresponding cells in more than one worksheet. You could enter your work onto one worksheet, then copy it onto the others, or you could group the worksheets and enter the standard text, data, formula and/or functions that will appear on them all. You then ungroup the sheets to add the elements that are unique to each one.

When worksheets are grouped, anything you do on one sheet is automatically replicated in every sheet in the group.

To group adjacent worksheets:

1 Click on the tab of the first sheet you want in the group.

2 Hold down [**Shift**] and click on the last tab in the group.

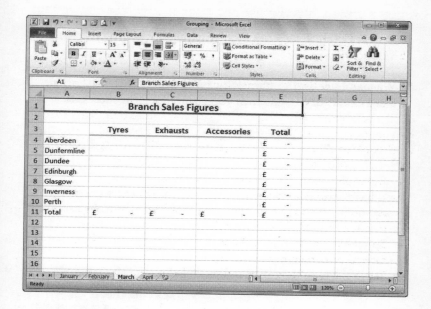

To group non-adjacent worksheets:

1 Click on the tab of the first sheet in the group.
2 Hold down [Ctrl] and click on each sheet tab that you want in the group.

To select all worksheets:

1 Right-click on any sheet tab.
2 Click Select all sheets.

When worksheets are grouped the word [Group] appears on the workbook title bar.

To ungroup worksheets:

1 Click on any worksheet tab that isn't part of the group.

Or

2 Right-click on one of the grouped worksheet tabs.
3 Choose Ungroup Sheets from the pop-up menu.

4.9 Tab colour

If you have several worksheets in a book (or related worksheets
across books) you may find colouring the sheet tabs to be useful.

To change the tab colour:
1 Select the tab(s) that you want to colour.
2 Right-click on the selected tabs and choose **Tab Color...**
3 Select a colour.

PROTECTING A WORKBOOK

If you want to ensure that others that share your workbook cannot
change the sheet names, tab colours or hide/unhide worksheets,
you must protect the structure of the workbook.

To protect the structure:
1 Display the **Review** tab.
2 Click **Protect Workbook** in the **Changes** group.
3 Select the **Protect Structure and Windows** options as required.

> ▷ Structure – sheet names, tab colours, sheet order, hide/unhide sheet options are disabled
> ▷ Window – window size and position cannot be adjusted when a workbook is open.

4 Add a password for added security and click **OK**.
5 Re-enter the password.
6 Click **OK**.
7 Save your workbook.

THINGS TO REMEMBER

1 *You can move between sheets in a workbook using the tabs.*

2 *The layout and design of a worksheet should be planned in advance.*

3 *Themes offer a quick way of styling sheets, and give consistent results.*

4 *Worksheets can be inserted, deleted, moved and copied or renamed, at any time as needed.*

5 *Sheets can be grouped for ease of handling.*

6 *You can hide/unhide workbooks.*

7 *You can change the tab colours.*

8 *To keep your workbook structure safe, you can turn on protection.*

TEST

1 *Where are the sheet navigation buttons?*

2 *What are the main objectives of good worksheet design?*

3 *What are the three theme elements?*

4 *What is the default number of worksheets when Excel is installed?*

5 *How can you change the default number of worksheets?*

6 *List three sheet management options.*

7 *Worksheets can only be moved and copied within a workbook – true or false?*

8 *What feature allows you to update/edit/format more than one worksheet at the same time?*

9 *In addition to sheet names, what other feature can help the user identify the worksheet required?*

10 *How can you protect the structure of your workbook so that other users cannot rename, move, add worksheets, etc.*

5

Formulas and functions

In this chapter you will learn:

- **more about functions and formulas**
- **about relative and absolute addresses and circular references**
- **how to use named ranges**
- **how to add comments and protect your worksheet**

Excel functions

Functions are pre-recorded formulas that you can use to make entering calculations simpler. Some functions are easy to understand – see the ones that follow. Others are a bit trickier – you might want to explore some of these later on, depending on what you want to use Excel for.

There are lots of different types of functions – statistical, financial, logical, text, database, lookup, date and time functions, etc. It is very unlikely that you will need to use them all (you'll be glad to know), but we'll look at some that are useful at a general level. You can then go on and explore the functions and find any that may be useful in your particular situation. Use the online Help as necessary.

5.1 AutoSum

The worksheet below contains details of quarterly sales figures. Enter the text and data into a new worksheet in your workbook.

We need to calculate the total sales figures for each sales representative for the year and also the total sales figure for each quarter.

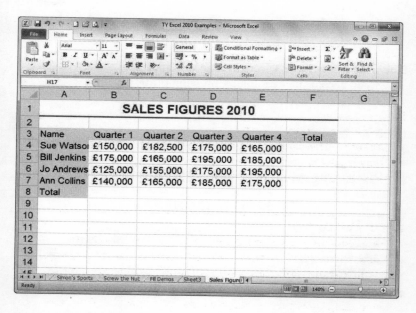

You could use a formula to calculate the total (e.g. in F4 you might have =B4+C4+D4+E4), but the easiest and quickest way to calculate it is with AutoSum.

To calculate the totals using AutoSum:

1 Select a cell to the right of a row or below a column of figures that you want to add, e.g. in cell F4 or cell B8.

2 Click the **AutoSum** button in the **Editing** group on the **Home** tab.

Or

■ Click the **AutoSum** button on the **Formulas** tab.

Σ AutoSum ▾

3 The range of cells to be added together will be highlighted. Note that the function also appears in the Formula bar.

4 If the suggested range of cells is correct, press [**Enter**].

Or

■ If the suggested range is not the range of cells you want to add, drag over the correct range, then press [**Enter**].

The total value of the selected range will appear in the active cell when you accept the formula by pressing [**Enter**].

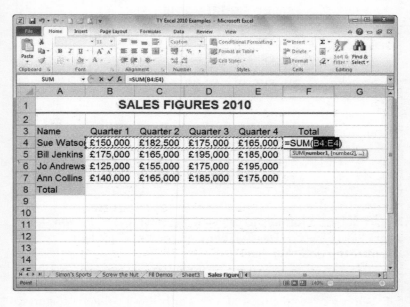

■ Excel calculates the total value of the selected cells using the SUM function. Its syntax is =SUM (cell range) – you could type in the function, but it's usually easier (and less error prone) to use AutoSum.

You could select each of the total cells in turn and use AutoSum to calculate the values that should appear in them, or use AutoFill (see section 2.11) to copy the function down or across the other total cells.

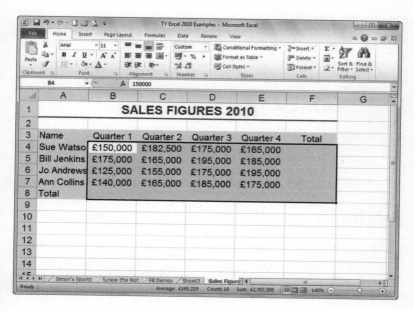

	A	B	C	D	E	F
1			SALES FIGURES 2010			
2						
3	Name	Quarter 1	Quarter 2	Quarter 3	Quarter 4	Total
4	Sue Watson	£150,000	£182,500	£175,000	£165,000	£ 672,500
5	Bill Jenkins	£175,000	£165,000	£195,000	£185,000	£ 720,000
6	Jo Andrews	£125,000	£155,000	£175,000	£195,000	£ 650,000
7	Ann Collins	£140,000	£165,000	£185,000	£175,000	£ 665,000
8	Total	£590,000	£667,500	£730,000	£720,000	£ 2,707,500
9						

To AutoSum several groups of cells simultaneously:

1 Select all of the rows and columns to total, and the cells to contain the results of the AutoSum calculations.

2 Click the **AutoSum** button.

Σ AutoSum ▾

The cells in the rightmost column and bottom row of the selected area will each have the Sum function inserted into them.

NON-ADJACENT CELLS

You can also use AutoSum to total non-adjacent cells if you wish.

To total non-adjacent cells:
1 Select the cell that will contain the result of the calculation.
2 Click the **AutoSum** button.
3 Click on the first cell you want to include in the range.
4 Hold down [**Ctrl**] and click on each of the other cells to be included in the function.
5 Press [**Enter**].

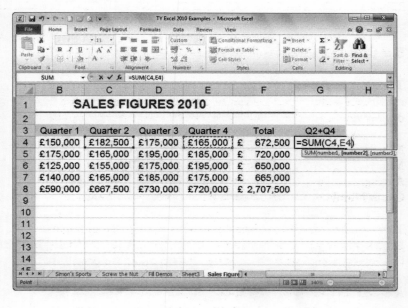

5.2 Common statistical functions

The most commonly used statistical functions – average, count, maximum and minimum – can be found in the AutoSum list. To display this, click the arrow on either of the AutoSum buttons.

Min	returns the smallest value
Max	returns the highest value
Average	returns the mean value (=total/count)
Count Numbers	returns the number of numeric entries.

There are lots of other statistical functions to be found in the Insert Function dialog box (see section 5.3). You can display the dialog box by clicking More Functions... at the bottom of the AutoSum list.

A useful statistical function not on the AutoSum list is CountA, which returns the number of numeric or text entries – it counts all cells that are not empty.

The Average, Count Numbers, CountA, Min and Max work in exactly the same way as the Sum function in the AutoSum list.

1 Select the cell that the result will be displayed in.
2 Choose the function required from the AutoSum list.
3 Drag over (or use [Ctrl]- **click** to select) the cells that the function will use.
4 Press [**Enter**].

Try them out on your Simon's Sports data. Display these values:

▶ *Minimum from the saving column.*
▶ *Maximum from the saving column.*
▶ *Number of items on sale.*
▶ *Average sale price of the items in the list.*

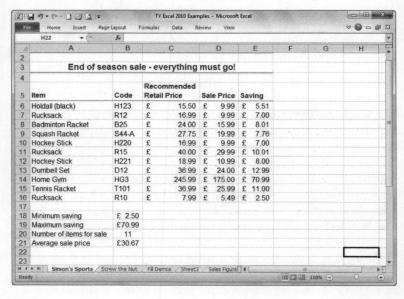

To edit a function:
1 Select the cell that contains the function.
2 Edit the function in the Formula bar.
Or
■ Click the **Insert Function** button again to display the **Function Arguments** dialog box.

Automatic summary data

When you select a range of cells that contains data, notice the summary calculations that appear automatically on the Status bar. The Average, Count and Sum are displayed.

5.3 Insert Function dialog box

To insert a function:
1 Select the cell that you want the function to go in.
2 Click the **Insert Function** button (to the left of the Formula bar).

Or
1 Click the drop-down arrow to the right of the **AutoSum** tool.
2 Select **More Functions...** from the list.

Or
1 Press [=].
2 Click the drop-down arrow at the top of the functions list.
3 Choose **More Functions...**
■ The **Insert Function** dialog box is displayed.

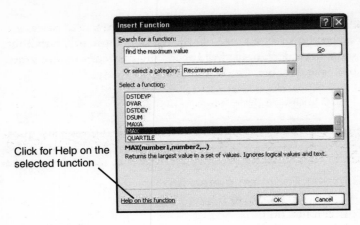

Click for Help on the
selected function

To search for a function:
1 Type what you want to do in the **Search for a function** field.
2 Click **Go**.
■ Excel will display a list of 'Recommended' functions.
3 Select a function from the list and click **OK**.

To select a function (without searching):
1 Select the category (choose **All** if you're not sure which one).
2 Scroll through the list to find the function.
3 Select it and click **OK**.
■ The **Function Arguments** dialog box appears.

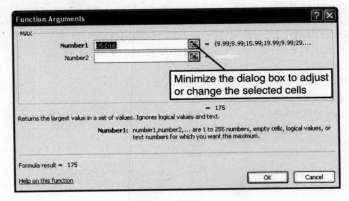

Minimize the dialog box to adjust
or change the selected cells

- If the **Function Arguments** dialog box obscures the area of the worksheet you want to view, click the button to the right of a data entry field – it will become minimized, so you can see your worksheet.
- To display the dialog box again, click the **Restore** button at the far right of the minimized window.

Restore

To edit a function:
1 Select the cell that contains the function.
2 Edit the function in the Formula bar.
Or
- Click the **Insert Function** button again to display the **Function Arguments** dialog box.

RECENTLY USED FUNCTIONS LIST

You can quickly add recently-used functions to the Formula bar using the Function list.

1 Select the cell where you want the function to go.
2 Type '='.
3 The **Name** box changes to a **Function list**.
4 Click the drop-down arrow to the right of the list.
5 Select the function required.
6 Complete the **Function Arguments** dialog box.
7 Click **OK**.
- **More Functions...** at the bottom of the list opens the **Insert Function** dialog box.

5.4 Show formulas

When setting up your worksheet, it is sometimes useful to display and print the formulas and functions that you have entered into the cells.

Each formula or function is displayed in the Formula bar when its cell is selected, but you can get Excel to display all the formulas and functions in your worksheet if you wish.

To switch the display of formulas and functions on and off:
  1 Display the **Formulas** tab on the Ribbon.
  2 Click the **Show Formulas** button in the **Formula Auditing** group.
Or
  ■ Use the keyboard shortcut [**Ctrl**]-[`] (at the top left of the keyboard, above [**Tab**]).

The formulas and functions used in the Simon's Sports worksheet are displayed below – note that what you can see is the data exactly as it is entered, and not as it is displayed on the screen.

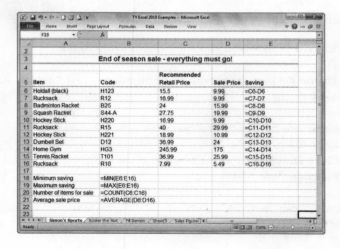

FORMULA AUTOCOMPLETE

If you opt to type your functions in, you can use **Formula AutoComplete** to help minimize typing and syntax errors. After you type an = (equal sign) and the first few letters of the function, a dynamic drop-down list of valid functions, names, and text strings will be displayed below the cell. You can select the one you want from the list – just click on it.

1 Type the = (equal sign) and start typing the function name.
■ As you type, a scrollable list of valid items is displayed with the closest match highlighted.
2 Click on the function required.
■ Detailed ScreenTips help you make the best choice.

The feature can be switched on or off in the **Options, Formulas** category, under **Working with Formulas**.

5.5 Formula Auditing

You can use the command buttons in the Formula Auditing groups to identify:

▶ *which cells are dependent on others, i.e. are calculated using values in other cells.*
▶ *which cell values are precedents, i.e. are used to calculate the values held in other cells.*

You can quickly trace the precedents and dependents of a cell using the Formula Auditing commands.

1. Select a cell that contains a formula or function.
2. Click the **Trace Precedents** button to identify which cells affect the value of the selected cell.
3. Click the **Trace Dependents** button to identify which cells are affected by the value in the selected cell.

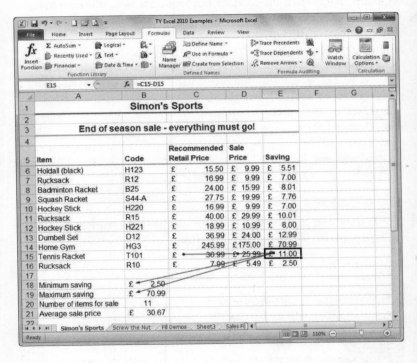

To remove the arrows:

- Click the drop-down arrow to the right of the **Remove Arrows** button and select from the options.

5.6 Relative and absolute addresses

You will have noticed that when you AutoFill or copy a formula, the addresses in it change automatically, relative to the position you copy them to. By default, the cell addresses used are relative addresses. There will be times when you use a cell address in a formula, and want to copy the formula down some rows or across some columns, but don't want the address to change relative to its new position.

In the next example, we are going to calculate the income from admissions to a film centre.

■ Enter the data onto a new worksheet (see section 4.4 to add a new sheet). DO NOT complete the Revenue columns – we will enter formulas to calculate those figures.

To calculate the January revenue figures:

1 Enter a formula into the Adult cell in the January, Revenue column to calculate the income from this group. The first revenue figure for January is calculated by multiplying the number of adults (B11) by the adult admission rate (D5). The formula in C11 should be =B11*D5.

2 Use AutoFill (see section 2.11) to copy the formula down over the OAP and Concession cells.

We could enter the appropriate formulas into the February and March columns in a similar way. However, it would be quicker to copy the January formulas. This poses two problems:

▶ *We don't want the D5 (adult rate), D6 (OAP rate), D7 (concession rate) addresses to change when we copy the formula.*

▶ *We can't use AutoFill because the cells we want to copy to are not next to the source cells.*

Absolute cell addresses

To stop a cell address in a formula or function from changing when the formula or function is copied or moved it must be fixed in some way so that it will not change.

By default cell addresses in formulas and functions are *relative* – which means that they update automatically when the formula or function is copied or moved – relative to the position that they are copied/moved to. To stop this happening you have to make the cell address(es) that you don't want to change *absolute*. This has the effect of locking the address – so that is doesn't change when the formula or function is copied or moved.

To create an absolute cell address:

■ Enter a $ sign in front of each coordinate you want to fix. Type the '$' sign, or use [F4].

Cell addresses in formulas and functions can be relative and/or absolute to different degrees, e.g.

$D$5	neither coordinate will change
D$5	the column will change if you copy the formula across columns
$D5	the row number will change if you copy the formula down rows
D5	both coordinates will change relative to its new position.

To absolutely address the cells in a formula:
1 Select the cell that contains the formula (e.g. C11) – the formula appears in the Formula bar.
2 Click in the Formula bar.
3 Place the insertion point within (or to the right) of the cell address you want to make absolute (e.g. D5).
4 Press [F4] until you have the cell addressed properly (or type $ in front of the coordinate(s)).

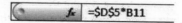

f_x =$D$5*B11

■ Each time you press [F4] it moves through the absolute addressing options.

Absolutely address the admission rate cell address in each of the January formulas.

Once you've made the appropriate addresses absolute, you can copy the formula across to the February and March columns.

To complete the February and March figures:
1 Select the cells you are copying from – the January revenue figures in this case, C11:C13.

2 Click the **Copy** button in the **Clipboard** group of the **Home** tab (or use [**Ctrl**]-[**C**]).

3 Select the first cell you want to paste into, e.g. E11 for the February figures – you don't need to select E11:E13.

4 Click the **Paste** button in the **Clipboard** group (or use [**Ctrl**]-[**V**]).

5 Select cell G11 as the first cell for the March figures.

6 Paste the data again.

7 Press [**Esc**] on your keyboard to cancel the copy routine.

Your final worksheet should look similar to the ones below and overleaf. The first picture displays the formulas (you may have different cell addresses if you have used different rows and columns for your data), the second one shows the results.

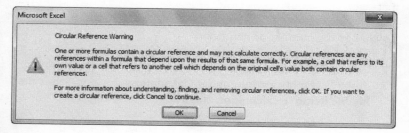

The spreadsheet shows:

SOUTHSIDE FILM CENTRE
MONTHLY INCOME FROM ADMISSIONS

Admission Charges	
Adult	£6.50
OAP	£4.00
Concessions	£3.50

	January		February		March	
	Number	Revenue	Number	Revenue	Number	Revenue
Adult	2500	£16,250.00	1950	£12,675.00	2400	£15,600.00
OAP	3400	£13,600.00	2750	£11,000.00	3200	£12,800.00
Consession	3950	£13,825.00	3500	£12,250.00	4300	£15,050.00

5.7 Circular references

If you create a formula that refers to its own cell (directly or indirectly), you create a circular reference. Excel cannot calculate open workbooks automatically if one of them has a circular reference in it.

When a circular reference occurs, Excel will display a dialog box alerting you to the problem.

Microsoft Excel

Circular Reference Warning

One or more formulas contain a circular reference and may not calculate correctly. Circular references are any references within a formula that depend upon the results of that same formula. For example, a cell that refers to its own value or a cell that refers to another cell which depends on the original cell's value both contain circular references.

For more information about understanding, finding, and removing circular references, click OK. If you want to create a circular reference, click Cancel to continue.

OK   Cancel

Click **OK** and read the Help page that appears, and minimize it so that you can refer back to it quickly if necessary.

To review and amend the circular references:
1 If you look at the Status bar, it will tell you where the circular reference is – if there is no cell address displayed, it means that the cell causing the problem is not on the current worksheet.

2 Go to the problem cell – click on it or go to the **Formula** tab, and in the **Formula Editing** group, click the arrow beside **Error Checking**, select **Circular References**, then the first cell reference displayed.

3 Check the formula and see if you can identify the problem. If the current cell address is in the formula, you have found the problem – amend it – no cell should contain a formula that refers to itself.

4 If you can't see the error, go to the next cell that is identified as being a problem cell.

5 Continue until you have located and fixed the error.

When the circular reference problem is resolved, the circular reference prompt will disappear from the status bar.

ITERATIONS

Some engineering and scientific formulas require circular references – in this case you may need to change the number of iterations (the number of times Excel recalculates the sheet) before giving an error message.

To change the number of iterations:
1 Click **File** to go to Backstage view.
2 Choose **Options** in the left panel.
3 In the **Formulas** section, under **Calculation Options**, select the **Enable iterative calculation** checkbox.

4 Type the number of iterations in the **Maximum** iterations box – the higher the number the more time Excel needs to calculate the worksheet.

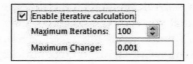

5 You can set the maximum amount of change you will accept in the **Maximum Change** box. The smaller the number, the more accurate the result, and the longer Excel needs to perform the calculation.

By default, Excel stops calculating after 100 iterations or after all values in the circular reference change by less than 0.001 between iterations – whichever comes first.

5.8 Named ranges

When building up your formulas and functions, you have been using cell addresses to tell Excel which cells you want to use in your calculations. Cell addresses are not really very user-friendly – it isn't always immediately clear what the formula =B13*$B$6 or the function =AVERAGE(D5:D17) is actually doing.

To make your worksheet easier to understand you can use named ranges instead of cell addresses in your formulas and functions.

There are two main ways of naming ranges.

You can either:

▶ *Use the existing labels that are on your worksheet to refer to the related data.*

Or

▶ *Create new descriptive names.*

CREATE NAMED RANGES

You can easily give a cell or range of cells a name. The name used can be anything you like (as long as it obeys the rules below) or you can use column and/or row labels as names for your cell ranges.

Rules for naming ranges

- The maximum size for a name is 255 characters.
- Spaces are not allowed (use an underscore or a full stop to separate words).
- The first character in a name must be a letter, backslash (\) or an underscore character
- Names can contain letters, numbers, full stops and underscores, but not commas, question marks or other punctuation characters.
- You cannot use a cell reference for a name, e.g. B75 or?AA$24.
- Names can contain upper and lower case letters. Excel is not case sensitive. If you create a name called Profit, then another called PROFIT, the second will replace the first.

To name cells using the existing row and column headings:
1 Select the row (or column) headings **and** the cells to be named.
2 Click **Create from Selection** in the **Defined Names** group.
3 Select the location of the names you wish to use in the **Create Names from Selection** dialog box.
4 Click **OK**.
- The scope of the named ranges is the workbook when you use this method.

To name a cell or range without using headings:
1 Select the cell or range of cells you want to name.
2 Click the **Name** box at the left edge of the Formula bar.
3 Type in a name for the cells.
4 Press [**Enter**].

- When you name cells in this way the scope of the named range is the workbook.

Or

1 Select the cells you want to name.
2 In the **Defined Names** group on the **Formula** tab, click the **Define Name** button (or drop down the **Define Name** options and choose **Define Name...**).

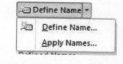

3 Enter the name to give the cell(s) in the Name field.
4 Specify the **Scope** of the named range – it could be the whole workbook, or a specific worksheet.
5 The range will be completed using the range of cells selected – edit if necessary.
6 Click **OK**.

If you limit the scope of a named range to a particular worksheet it will only be available in that worksheet.

You could try naming ranges for:

▶ *the columns in the Screw the Nut plc worksheet.*
▶ *the admission charges in the Film Centre worksheet, with names such as Adult_rate, OAP_rate, and Con_rate.*

You can easily paste names into your formula or function, rather than using the cell addresses.

To use a name in a formula or function:

1 Select the cell that will contain your formula or function.
2 Start entering the formula or function in the normal way.

3 When you want to specify the range that you wish to use, click the **Use in Formula** button in the **Defined Names** group and select the name from the list.

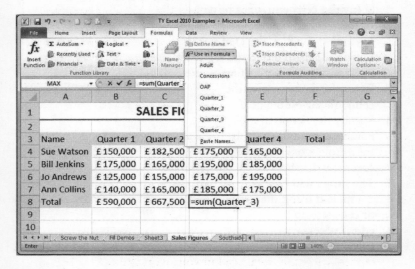

- Edit some formulas to use range names instead of addresses.

If you no longer use a name, you can delete it. Deleting the name does not delete the cell contents, but it will affect any cells that refer to the name in a formula.

To delete a name:
  1 Click **Name Manager** in the **Defined Names** group.
  2 Select the name you no longer require.
  3 Click **Delete**.
  4 You will be prompted to confirm the deletion – click **OK**.
  5 Close the **Name Manager** dialog box.

Author's insight

If you delete a named range that is used in a formula, this

error message is displayed in the cell. `#NAME?`

You can check out the options for dealing with the error using the Smart tag that appears to the left of the cell – and **Invalid Name Error** is obviously the problem.

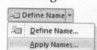

Amend the formula or function to reference the appropriate cell address again.

APPLYING NAMES

If you have created your formulas using cell addresses, and then decide to use named ranges, you can easily convert the addresses to range names.

To use this feature, the scope of the named range must be the worksheet.

1 To convert all of the cell addresses in your formulas to named ranges, select any single cell in your worksheet.
Or

To convert only part of your worksheet, select the range.
2 Choose **Apply Names…** from the **Define Name** drop-down list.
3 Select the names you want to apply.
4 Click **OK**.

Experiment with names – they are really handy as they can make your worksheets much easier to understand.

The Sales Figures worksheet below was updated by creating names, then using the Apply Names feature.

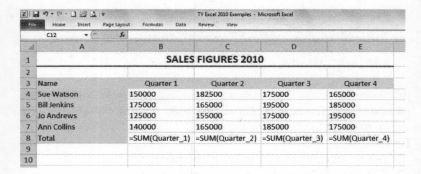

You can also edit a name from the **Name Manager** dialog box.

5.9 Comments

If you think that the purpose of a formula in a cell is not self-explicit, you can add a note – called a 'comment' – to the cell. You will find them particularly useful if you don't use named ranges, and want to add an explanation to a cell, or, if others share your worksheets and you want to explain the logic behind an entry you have made.

To add a comment to a cell:
1 Select the cell you want to add a comment to.
2 On the **Review** tab on the Ribbon, click **New Comment** in the **Comments** group.
3 Type your comment into the comment box.
4 Click outside the box. A small red triangle will appear in the top right corner of your cell to indicate that it has a comment attached.

To edit an existing comment:
1 Select the cell that the comment is attached to.
2 Click the **Edit Comment** button in the **Comments** group.

Edit   Delete   Show/Hide

Previous   Next

3 Edit the text and click outside the box.

To delete a comment:
1 Select the cell that the comment is attached to.
2 Click the **Delete** button in the **Comments** group.

If your worksheet contains several comments, you can move
through your worksheet, jumping from one comment to the next
using the **Previous** and **Next** buttons.

If you want a comment to remain visible on your screen when you
move off the cell that it is attached to:
1 Select the cell.
2 Click the **Show/Hide Comment** button to toggle the display.

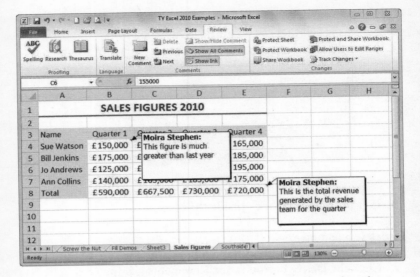

The name that appears automatically in a comment is taken from the user name in the Excel Options. You can edit or delete the name in the comment if you wish.

If you want all comments displayed:
■ Click the **Show All Comments** button (click it again to hide them all).

To format a comment:
1 Show the comment.
2 Go to the **Home** tab, select the comment, then click the drop-down arrow beside **Format in the Cells** group, and choose **Format Comment** from the options.

Or
▶ Select the comment and press [**Ctrl**]-[**1**].
3 Format the lines and/or fill using the options on the **Colors and Lines** tab.
4 Click **OK**.

5.10 Worksheet protection

Having gone to the trouble of setting up formulas and functions on your worksheet, it would be a pity if they were accidentally overwritten when entering text and data. You can protect your worksheet to avoid this unfortunate situation arising.

When you protect a worksheet, cells formatted as **locked** cannot be edited, cells formatted as **unlocked** can. Initially all cells are locked. You must therefore unlock cells that you want to be able to edit in the protected sheet, before you protect the sheet.

You may sometimes want to hide your formulas – especially if others are using the worksheets. If cells are formatted as **hidden**, the formula does not appear in the Formula bar when the cell is selected, or when the sheet is in Formula view once the worksheet protection has been activated.

To unlock cells:
  1 Select the cells that you want unlocked.
  2 On the **Home** tab, in the **Cells** group, click **Format**.
  3 Click **Lock Cell** under the **Protection** options to unlock the selected cells. The **Lock Cell** tool is a toggle.

To hide cell formulas:
  1 Select the cells whose formulas you want to hide.
  2 On the **Home** tab, in the **Cells** group, click **Format**, then **Format Cells**.

3 Select the **Protection** tab.

4 Tick the **Hidden** checkbox.

To activate the protection:

1 In the **Cells** group on the **Home** tab, click **Format**, then **Protect Sheet...**

2 If you wish to give your protection a password, enter it in the dialog box – just don't forget it!

3 Select the options you want made available to the user.

4 Click **OK**.

5 If you have given a password, re-enter it at the prompt and click **OK** again.

To deactivate the protection:

1 In the **Cells** group of the **Home** tab, click **Format**, then **Unprotect Sheet...**

2 If you used a password, enter it at the prompt.

3 Click **OK**.

Author's insight

This is another example of why you might want to protect a worksheet.

We discussed protecting worksheets in Chapter 4, where we wanted to protect the *structure* of the worksheet, rather than the formulas and functions within it.

THINGS TO REMEMBER

1 *The most commonly used functions include AutoSum, Sum, Min, Max, Average, Count and CountA.*

2 *You can insert and define function using the Insert Function dialog box.*

3 *You can make the worksheet display the formulas instead of their results.*

4 *The formula auditing tools will help you to solve problems.*

5 *Addresses can be relative or absolute.*

6 *A formula may use the value in a cell which is changed by the formula. This is a circular reference. It may be intentional, or a mistake!*

7 *You can create names to use in place of addresses. They make formulas more readable. Comments can be added to cells to explain their contents.*

8 *You can protecting the contents of your worksheet from accidental damage.*

9 *Cells can be locked so their contents cannot be changed.*

10 *Formulas can be hidden, if required.*

TEST

Look carefully at this worksheet. What function is in cell:

1 F2
2 G8
3 H11
4 C20
5 D21
6 E22
7 C23
8 G20
9 G21
10 G22

	A	B	C	D	E	F	G	H
1	Firstname	Surname	Computing %	Maths %	English %			
2	Gill	McLaren	45	60	70	70	45	58
3	Pauline	Watson	65	88	80	88	65	78
4	William	Smith	72	76	55	76	55	68
5	Ann	Allan	48	82	84	84	48	71
6	Andrew	Borthwick	52	65	76	76	52	64
7	Peter	Jackson	91	49	83	91	49	74
8	Alison	Smith	50	55	57	57	50	54
9	Marion	Williamson	49	89	65	89	49	68
10	Hector	Smith	85	49	74	85	49	69
11	David	Watson	59	66	65	66	59	63
12	Alice	Graham	65	58	82	82	58	68
13	Belinda	Williamson	75	75	45	75	45	65
14	Colin	Taylor	45	92	88	92	45	75
15	Derek	Cunningham	80	65	55	80	55	67
16	Elaine	Nelson	39	77	88	88	39	68
17	Frances	Watson	57	69	44	69	44	57
18	Gregory	Young	63	80	70	80	63	71
19								
20			91	92	88		92	
21			39	49	44		39	
22			61	70	69		67	
23			17					
24								

6

More functions

In this chapter you will learn:

- *about Logical, Statistical, Math, Text, Date and Financial functions*
- *how to use Lookup tables*
- *about data tables, scenarios and PivotTables*

6.1 Logical functions

IF FUNCTION

The IF function is used to return one value if the condition you specify is True, and another value if the condition is False. The values returned can be text, numbers, or the result of a formula or function.

For example, you might be entering student end-of-term exam results into your worksheet. If a student has 50% or more in the exam, a pass will be awarded, if less than 50% is achieved, the result is a fail.

COMPARISON OPERATORS

Comparison operators are used in many functions. The next example uses one to check if the Total Mark is greater than or equal to 50. The operators include:

=	equal to	<>	not equal to
>	greater than	>=	greater than or equal to
<	less than	<=	less than or equal to

Enter this data into a new worksheet.

	A	B	C	D	E
1	**END OF TERM EXAM RESULTS**				
2					
3	**Firstname**	**Surname**	**Mark awarded**	**Result**	**Grade**
4	Gill	McLaren	45		
5	Pauline	Watson	65		
6	William	Smith	72		
7	Ann	Allan	48		
8	Andrew	Borthwick	52		
9	Peter	Jackson	91		
10	Alison	Smith	50		
11	Marion	Williamson	49		
12	Hector	Smith	68		
13	David	Watson	59		
14					

To return a 'Pass' or 'Fail' message in the Result column, we need to enter the IF function. You can use either cell addresses or named ranges in the function. In this example, the C4:C13 range has been named *Mark_awarded*.

To enter the function:

1 Select the first cell in the result column.
2 On the **Formulas** tab, click **Logical** in the **Function Library**.
3 Select **IF**.

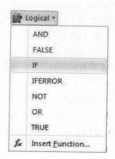

4 In the **Function Arguments** dialog box, enter the condition to be evaluated in the **Logical test** field (Mark_awarded>=50).

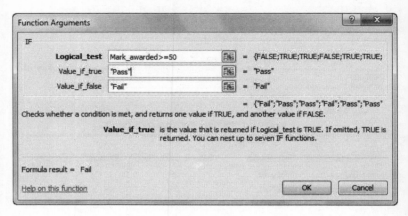

5 Specify the value if the condition is found to be True – you don't need to type in the quotes – Excel will enter them automatically as it builds the formula.
6 Specify the value if the condition is found to be False.
7 Click **OK**.

Arguments

The values used by functions to perform calculations or operations are called arguments.

An argument may be a numeric value, a text value, a cell reference, a range of cells, a named range, or a nested function (a function within a function, see 'Nested Ifs' below).

- AutoFill the function down through the *Result* column – 'Pass' will appear in the rows where the condition is true, 'Fail' will appear in the rows where the condition is false.

	D4		▼	fx	=IF(Mark_awarded>=50,"Pass","Fail")

	A	B	C	D	E
1	**END OF TERM EXAM RESULTS**				
2					
3	**Firstname**	**Surname**	**Mark awarded**	**Result**	
4	Gill	McLaren	45	Fail	
5	Pauline	Watson	65	Pass	
6	William	Smith	72	Pass	
7	Ann	Allan	48	Fail	
8	Andrew	Borthwick	52	Pass	
9	Peter	Jackson	91	Pass	
10	Alison	Smith	50	Pass	
11	Marion	Williamson	49	Fail	
12	Hector	Smith	68	Pass	
13	David	Watson	59	Pass	
14					

With the formulas displayed, the worksheet should look like the
illustration below. This example uses named ranges rather than cell
addresses. If we had used cell addresses the function would have
been =IF(C4>=50, "PASS", "FAIL"), etc.

	E13		▼	fx	

	A	B	C	D
1	**END OF TERM EXAM RESULTS**			
2				
3	**Firstname**	**Surname**	**Mark awarded**	**Result**
4	Gill	McLaren	45	=IF(Mark_awarded>=50,"Pass","Fail")
5	Pauline	Watson	65	=IF(Mark_awarded>=50,"Pass","Fail")
6	William	Smith	72	=IF(Mark_awarded>=50,"Pass","Fail")
7	Ann	Allan	48	=IF(Mark_awarded>=50,"Pass","Fail")
8	Andrew	Borthwick	52	=IF(Mark_awarded>=50,"Pass","Fail")
9	Peter	Jackson	91	=IF(Mark_awarded>=50,"Pass","Fail")
10	Alison	Smith	50	=IF(Mark_awarded>=50,"Pass","Fail")
11	Marion	Williamson	49	=IF(Mark_awarded>=50,"Pass","Fail")
12	Hector	Smith	68	=IF(Mark_awarded>=50,"Pass","Fail")
13	David	Watson	59	=IF(Mark_awarded>=50,"Pass","Fail")

NESTED IFS

This next example illustrates nested IFs. We are going to add another column to our worksheet to give the Grade achieved by each student. We need to use the IF function to check the Total Mark and return the appropriate grade.

- ▶ *IF a student gets 70% or more the grade is an A.*
- ▶ *IF the student gets 60% to 69% the grade is a B.*
- ▶ *IF the student gets 50% to 59% the grade is a C.*
- ▶ *Less than 50% is a fail.*

As we have four possible outcomes (not just a Pass or Fail) we must nest our IF functions to work through the various options.

1 Add a new column heading, 'Grade', in the column to the right of the Result column.
2 Select the first cell in the Grade column.
3 On the **Formulas** tab, click **Logical** in the **Function Library** and select **IF**.
4 In the **Function Arguments** dialog box, enter the condition that you want to be evaluated in the Logical test field (Mark_awarded>=70 in this case) and specify the **Value if true** – A (70% and over gets an A).
5 In the **Value if false** field, click **IF** at the top of the **Regularly used functions** list (left end of the Formula bar).
6 Complete the next set of conditions and values. Enter the condition that you want to be evaluated in the **Logical test** field (Mark_awarded>=60), and specify the **Value if true** – B (60%–69% gets a B grade).

7 In the **Value if false** field, click the **IF** at the top of the
   Regularly used functions list.
8 Enter the **Logical test** – Mark_awarded>=50.
9 Specify the **Value if true** – C (50%–59% gets a C grade) and
   the **Value if false** – Fail.
10 Click **OK**.
11 AutoFill the functions down the column.

	E4		f_x "Fail"}))		
	A	B	C	D	E
1			**END OF TERM EXAM RESULTS**		
2					
3	**Firstname**	**Surname**	**Mark awarded**	**Result**	**Grade**
4	Gill	McLaren	45	Fail	Fail
5	Pauline	Watson	65	Pass	B
6	William	Smith	72	Pass	A
7	Ann	Allan	48	Fail	Fail
8	Andrew	Borthwick	52	Pass	C
9	Peter	Jackson	91	Pass	A
10	Alison	Smith	50	Pass	C
11	Marion	Williamson	49	Fail	Fail
12	Hector	Smith	68	Pass	B
13	David	Watson	59	Pass	C
14					
15					

| ◄ ◄ ► ► | Alignment | Sales Figures | Southside Film Centre | **Student Results** | |

Ready | | | | Count: 10 |

You should get A, B, C and Fail grades as appropriate. If the function does not work as expected, delete it and try again.

In this next example, the IF function is used to work out the amount of discount a customer will get on an order.

- If the order is £1000 or over, 10% will be deducted.
- If the order is between £750 and £999, 5% will be deducted.
- If the order is less than £750, no discount is given.

Enter the basic worksheet as it is displayed here. The empty columns will be completed using functions and formulas.

Named ranges have been created for the columns, using the Name Box.

- The Value of order column has been called VOO.
- The Discount column has been called Discount.
- The Net Amount column has been called Net_Amount.
- The VAT column has been called VAT.

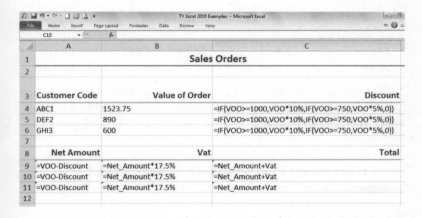

A	B	C	D	E	F
Sales Orders					
Customer Code	**Value of Order**	**Discount**	**Net Amount**	**Vat**	**Total**
ABC1	£1,523.75	£ 152.38	£1,371.38	£ 239.99	£1,611.37
DEF2	£ 890.00	£ 44.50	£ 845.50	£ 147.96	£ 993.46
GHI3	£ 600.00	£ -	£ 600.00	£ 105.00	£ 705.00

These names have been used in the functions and formulas. The formulas and functions required are shown in the next screenshot.

A	B	C
Sales Orders		
Customer Code	Value of Order	Discount
ABC1	1523.75	=IF(VOO>=1000,VOO*10%,IF(VOO>=750,VOO*5%,0))
DEF2	890	=IF(VOO>=1000,VOO*10%,IF(VOO>=750,VOO*5%,0))
GHI3	600	=IF(VOO>=1000,VOO*10%,IF(VOO>=750,VOO*5%,0))
Net Amount	**Vat**	**Total**
=VOO-Discount	=Net_Amount*17.5%	=Net_Amount+Vat
=VOO-Discount	=Net_Amount*17.5%	=Net_Amount+Vat
=VOO-Discount	=Net_Amount*17.5%	=Net_Amount+Vat

AND

The AND function returns a TRUE result if all conditions in the function are met, and a FALSE result if all conditions are not met.

For example, you may manufacture and sell traditional wooden toys. Your most popular items are a painted toy box, a rocking horse and building blocks. You want to keep a record of the items that customers buy from you, so that you can see at a glance who has bought at least one of each of these items.

	A	B	C	D	E
	E3	▼	f_x		
1	Customer Purchase Data				
2	Customer	Painted Toy Box	Rocking Horse	Building Blocks	Bought each item
3	Jill Johnston	2	1	2	
4	Peter Jack	0	1	2	
5	Bart Simpson	1	1	4	
6	Ann Black	1	0	1	
7					

You could enter the data into a spreadsheet and use AND to return a TRUE value if a customer buys >o of each item, and FALSE if they don't. In this example, you would create the function in E3 like this:

1 Click the **Logical function** button in the **Function Library** group on the **Formulas** tab.
2 Choose **AND** from the list.
3 In the **Logical1** field, enter B3>o.
4 In the **Logical2** field, enter C3>o.
5 In the **Logical3** field, enter D3>o.
6 Click **OK**.

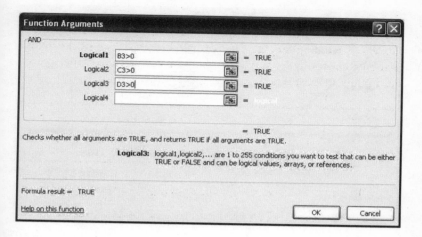

When you copy (AutoFill) the function down the column, you will get a TRUE message where ALL the conditions are met and a FALSE message where they are not.

OR

The OR function will return a TRUE value if any condition in the function is met, and FALSE if none are met.

You could add another column to the example used above to identify customers who have bought more than two of any item that we sell.

1 Click the **Logical function** button in the **Function Library** group on the **Formulas** tab.
2 Choose **OR** from the list.
3 In the **Logical1** field, enter B3>2 to check if the value in B3 is greater than 2.
4 In the **Logical2** field, enter C3>2.
5 In the **Logical3** field, enter D3>2.
6 Click **OK**.

Function Arguments ?×

OR

Logical1	B3>2	📷	= FALSE
Logical2	C3>2	📷	= FALSE
Logical3	D3>2|	📷	= FALSE
Logical4		📷	= logical

= FALSE

Checks whether any of the arguments are TRUE, and returns TRUE or FALSE. Returns FALSE only if all arguments are FALSE.

Logical3: logical1,logical2,... are 1 to 255 conditions that you want to test that can be either TRUE or FALSE.

Formula result = FALSE

Help on this function   [OK] [Cancel]

When you copy the function down the column, you will get a TRUE message where any condition is met and a FALSE message where none are.

| F3 | fx =OR(B3>2,C3>2,D3>2) |

	A	B	C	D	E	F
1	**Customer Purchase Data**					
2	Customer	Painted Toy Box	Rocking Horse	Building Blocks	Bought each item	Bought more than 2 of any item
3	Jill Johnston	2	1	2	TRUE	FALSE
4	Peter Jack	0	1	2	FALSE	FALSE
5	Bart Simpson	1	1	4	TRUE	TRUE
6	Ann Black	1	0	1	FALSE	FALSE
7						

Author's insight

You can combine IFs and ANDs and ORs in a variety of ways.

You could use a combination of IF and AND to identify those customers who had bought at least one of each item,

and display a message saying that they qualify for a free
Teddy Bear, or perform a calculation to give a 5% discount.

Your Function Arguments would look something like the next
screenshot – with the AND function nested within an IF.

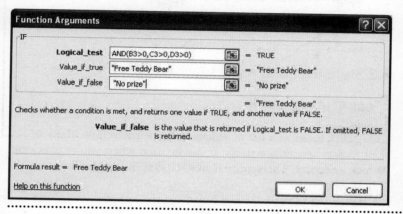

OTHER LOGICAL FUNCTIONS

NOT   This reverses the logic of a function, e.g. the function
              =AND(B3>0,C3>0,D3>0) in E3 at the bottom
              of page 143 gives a TRUE outcome – the customer
              has bought at least one of each item. If you change
              the function to =NOT(AND(B3>0,C3>0,D3>0)) it
              means that you are looking for a TRUE outcome
              when the customer has not bought at least one of
              each item.

IFERROR   This function returns a message that you specify if
              the formula or function in the cell gives an error.
              In the example below, the result in A13 will be 40.
              If you change the 5 to a 0, an error occurs because
              you cannot divide something by zero – and the
              message **Error in formula** will be displayed.

10	200
11	5
12	
13	=IFERROR(A10/A11,"Error in formula")

6.2 Statistical and math functions

COUNTIF AND SUMIF

COUNTIF looks at a list of values and calculates how many of them satisfy specified criteria. It can be used when you're checking for one criterion. The syntax is =COUNTIF(Range,Criteria)

1 Click the **Insert Function** button at the left of the Formula bar (or on the **Formulas** tab).
2 Select the COUNTIF function (you'll find it in the Statistical or All categories).

3 Enter the range of cells that you want to be counted in the Range field.

4 Specify the criteria that must be met for an entry to be counted in the Criteria field.

5 Click **OK**.

The function could be used to count the number of students that obtained specific results in their exams.

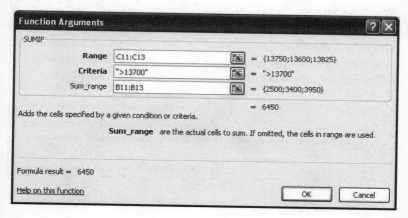

	A	B	C	D	E	F	G	H
	G12	▼	*fx*					
1			**END OF TERM EXAM RESULTS**					
2								
3	**Firstname**	**Surname**	**Mark awarded**	**Result**	**Grade**			
4	Gill	McLaren	45	Fail	Fail		No of students with	
5	Pauline	Watson	65	Pass	B		>=80	1
6	William	Smith	72	Pass	A			
7	Ann	Allan	48	Fail	Fail		No of students with	
8	Andrew	Borthwick	52	Pass	C		<50	3
9	Peter	Jackson	91	Pass	A			
10	Alison	Smith	50	Pass	C			
11	Marion	Williamson	49	Fail	Fail			
12	Hector	Smith	68	Pass	B			
13	David	Watson	59	Pass	C			

The SUMIF function (in the Math & Trig category) works in a similar way to COUNTIF, but adds the values together if the condition is met.

Function Arguments

SUMIF

Range	C11:C13		= {13750;13600;13825}
Criteria	">13700"		= ">13700"
Sum_range	B11:B13		= {2500;3400;3950}

= 6450

Adds the cells specified by a given condition or criteria.

Sum_range are the actual cells to sum. If omitted, the cells in range are used.

Formula result = 6450

Help on this function   OK   Cancel

The Range is the range of cells you want evaluated.

The Criteria specify the conditions you want to check for.

Sum_range is the range of cells to add together. If this is left blank, the cells identified in the Range field will be added.

> ### Author's insight
> Wildcard characters
>
> You can use *wildcard* characters in COUNTIF and SUMIF functions.
>
> A ? can be used to represent a single character.
>
> An * is used to represent a string of characters.
>
> Entering **=COUNTIF(B4:B13,"W*")** in a cell will count the number of values in cell range B4:B13, where the entry starts with W and is followed by any number of characters.
>
> See COUNTIF and SUMIF in the online Help for more examples.

6.3 Text functions

There are a number of text functions that you may find useful from time to time. They are very easy to use. You could type up a list of names and experiment using the functions discussed.

	A	B	C	D	E	F
				Full Name in	Full Name in	Full Name with
1	Firstname	Surname	Full Name	UPPER case	LOWER Case	Initial Capitals
2	Gill	Mclaren				
3	Peter	Shaw				
4	Kim	Stephen				
5	Andrew	Borthwick				
6	Alison	Peterson				
7	Amanda	Mitchell				
8	Gordon	Williamson				
9	Clare	Stephen				
10	Jack	Williamson				
11	Ann	Shaw				
12	Alison	Anderson				

CONCATENATE

The CONCATENATE function joins text together. In this example it displays the full name in column C.

1 Click the **Text** button in the **Function Library** group on the **Formulas** tab.
2 Select the **Concatenate** function.
3 Enter the cell address that contains the first piece of text required in Text1.

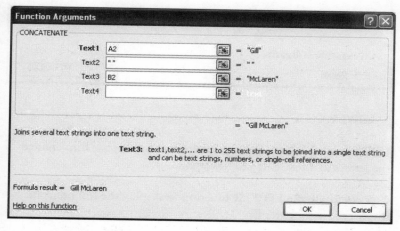

4 Put a space – this could be any character – in Text2 (in quotation marks). If you don't put in a space, the words will run together.
5 Enter the cell address that contains the next piece of text required in Text3.
6 Continue until all text strings have been entered – you can have up to 30 text strings.
7 Click **OK**.

UPPER

UPPER is a case change function. You can use it to change the letters in a text entry to upper case. You could use the UPPER function to display the full name in upper case in Column D.

1 Click the **Text** button in the **Function Library** group on the **Formulas** tab.
2 Select the **UPPER** function.
3 Enter the cell address that contains the text you want to convert, e.g. C2.
4 Click **OK**.

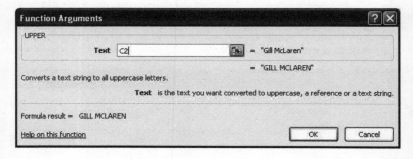

LOWER

LOWER is also a case change function. You can use it to change the letters in a text entry to lower case.

You could use the LOWER function to display the full name in lower case in Column E.

1 Click the **Text** button in the **Function Library** group on the **Formulas** tab.
2 Select the **LOWER** function.
3 Enter the cell address that contains the text you want to convert, e.g. C2.
4 Click **OK**.

PROPER

PROPER converts a text entry to initial capitals. You could use it to display the name with initial capitals in Column F.

1 Click the **Text** button in the **Function Library** group on the **Formulas** tab.

2 Select the **PROPER** function.
3 Enter the cell address that contains the text you want to convert, e.g. C2.
4 Click **OK**.

	A	B	C	D	E	F
				Full Name in UPPER case	**Full Name in LOWER Case**	**Full Name with Initial Capitals**
1	**Firstname**	**Surname**	**Full Name**			
2	Gill	McLaren	=CONCATENATE(A2," ",B2)	=UPPER(C2)	=LOWER(C2)	=PROPER(C2)
3	Peter	Shaw	=CONCATENATE(A3," ",B3)	=UPPER(C3)	=LOWER(C3)	=PROPER(C3)
4	Kim	Stephen	=CONCATENATE(A4," ",B4)	=UPPER(C4)	=LOWER(C4)	=PROPER(C4)
5	Andrew	Borthwick	=CONCATENATE(A5," ",B5)	=UPPER(C5)	=LOWER(C5)	=PROPER(C5)
6	Alison	Peterson	=CONCATENATE(A6," ",B6)	=UPPER(C6)	=LOWER(C6)	=PROPER(C6)
7	Amanda	Mitchell	=CONCATENATE(A7," ",B7)	=UPPER(C7)	=LOWER(C7)	=PROPER(C7)
8	Gordon	Williamson	=CONCATENATE(A8," ",B8)	=UPPER(C8)	=LOWER(C8)	=PROPER(C8)
9	Clare	Stephen	=CONCATENATE(A9," ",B9)	=UPPER(C9)	=LOWER(C9)	=PROPER(C9)
10	Jack	Williamson	=CONCATENATE(A10," ",B10)	=UPPER(C10)	=LOWER(C10)	=PROPER(C10)
11	Ann	Shaw	=CONCATENATE(A11," ",B11)	=UPPER(C11)	=LOWER(C11)	=PROPER(C11)
12	Alison	Anderson	=CONCATENATE(A12," ",B12)	=UPPER(C12)	=LOWER(C12)	=PROPER(C12)
13						

6.4 Date functions

Date functions allow you to insert the current date and/or time into a cell on your worksheet (or into calculations), and display the date and/or time in a variety of ways.

TODAY()

The TODAY() function enters the date from your computer clock into your worksheet. It's such a regularly used function that most people enter it directly through the keyboard.

To insert the current day:
1 Select a cell in your worksheet.
2 Type in =TODAY() – you must type in the = and the () to get the function to work.
3 Press [Enter].
Or
1 Click the **Date & Time** button in the **Function Library** group on the **Formulas** tab.

2 Choose **Today** from the list.

3 Click **OK**.

NOW()

The NOW() function enters the date and time from your computer clock. Again, it is usually typed in through the keyboard.

To insert the current day:

1 Select a cell in your worksheet.

2 Type in =NOW() – you must type in the = and the ().

3 Press [**Enter**].

Or

1 Click the **Date & Time** button in the **Function Library** group on the **Formulas** tab.

2 Choose **Now** from the list.

3 Click **OK**.

If the NOW() function does not display as a Date and Time, display the **Format Cells** dialog box, choose the '**Custom**' category on the **Number** tab, and select a **Date and Time** format.

If the date and/or time are not correct when you use these functions you will need to reset the clock on your computer.

The values in the cells with the TODAY() or NOW() function in them are volatile. The TODAY() function will be updated automatically. The NOW() function will be updated each time the worksheet is recalculated – click the **Calculate Now** command button in the **Calculation** group (or press [**F9**]).

DAY, MONTH AND YEAR

The DAY, MONTH and YEAR functions can be used to display just the section of the date required. You can use the function to return the portion required from a date entered into a cell in your worksheet, or you can nest the TODAY or NOW function within it.

To return part of a date already in a cell:

1 Select the cell that you want the DAY, MONTH or YEAR displayed in.

2 Click the **Date & Time** command button.

3 Choose DAY, MONTH or YEAR from the function list.

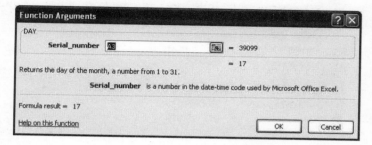

4 Enter the cell address in the **Serial_Number** field.

5 Click **OK**.

To enter part of a date from a TODAY() or NOW() function:

1 Select the cell that you want the DAY, MONTH or YEAR in.

2 Click the **Date & Time** button.

3 Choose DAY, MONTH or YEAR from the function list.

4 Type TODAY() or NOW() in the **Serial_Number** field.

5 Click **OK**.

The TODAY() and NOW() functions are useful when calculating things like age, length of service, or the length of time an item has been in stock.

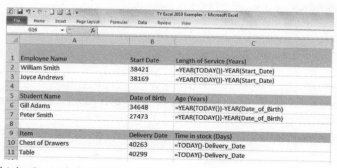

Using Date functions to calculate lengths of time: the formulas...

	A	B	C
1	**Employee Name**	**Start Date**	**Length of Service (Years)**
2	William Smith	10/03/2005	5
3	Joyce Andrews	01/07/2004	6
4			
5	**Student Name**	**Date of Birth**	**Age (Years)**
6	Gill Adams	10/11/1994	16
7	Peter Smith	20/03/1975	35
8			
9	**Item**	**Delivery Date**	**Time in stock (Days)**
10	Chest of Drawers	26/03/2010	72
11	Table	01/05/2010	36

... and the resulting values

DATEDIF

A useful date function not found in the online Help is =DATEDIF.

DATEDIF calculates the amount of time between two given dates using the syntax **=DATEDIF(Date1, Date2, OutputRequirement)**

Date 1 is the earlier of the dates you are using

Date 2 is the later of the dates you are using

OutputRequirement is a code that specifies the type of output required e.g. years, months or days.

Code	Description	Result
"d"	Days	Number of days between Date1 and Date2
"m"	Months	Number of complete months between Date1 and Date2
"y"	Years	Number of complete years between Date1 and Date2

Code	Description	Result
"md"	Days excluding Months and Years	Number of days between Date1 and Date2, as if Date1 and Date2 were in the same month and the same year
"yd"	Days excluding Years	Number of days between Date1 and Date2, as if Date1 and Date2 were in the same year
"ym"	Months excluding Years	Number of months between Date1 and Date2, as if Date1 and Date2 were in the same year

This function is ideally suited to calculating someone's precise age on any particular date. You can combine it with text functions to display a narrative showing the calculation, e.g.

=DATEDIF(DOB,TODAY(),"y")&" years"&DATEDIF(DOB,TODAY(),"ym")&" months"&DATEDIF(DOB,TODAY(),"md")&" days"

Where DOB is a named range for cells B24:B27 and Today() is picking up today's date from the computer.

		DOB	Age
17			
18		**DOB**	**Age**
19	Joe	01 April 1987	**23 years 2 months 5 days**
20	Ann	04 September 1975	**34 years 9 months 2 days**
21	Bill	21 July 2006	**3 years 10 months 16 days**
22	Elke	27 October 1993	**16 years 7 months 10 days**
23			

		DOB	Age
17			
18		DOB	Age
19	Joe	31868	=DATEDIF(DOB,TODAY(),"y")&" years "&DATEDIF(DOB,TODAY(),"ym")&" months "&DATEDIF(DOB,TODAY(),"md")&" days"
20	Ann	27641	=DATEDIF(DOB,TODAY(),"y")&" years "&DATEDIF(DOB,TODAY(),"ym")&" months "&DATEDIF(DOB,TODAY(),"md")&" days"
21	Bill	38919	=DATEDIF(DOB,TODAY(),"y")&" years "&DATEDIF(DOB,TODAY(),"ym")&" months "&DATEDIF(DOB,TODAY(),"md")&" days"
22	Elke	34269	=DATEDIF(DOB,TODAY(),"y")&" years "&DATEDIF(DOB,TODAY(),"ym")&" months "&DATEDIF(DOB,TODAY(),"md")&" days"
23			

6.5 Financial functions

Out of the many financial functions in Excel, those dealing with loans and investments are perhaps the ones that are most useful to us all, at a personal if not professional level. Three deal with the repayment of loans (which we all have to handle at some time!), and two are useful when working with savings and investments. The arguments used in these functions are:

pv   the present (original) value of the loan
pmt   the repayment per period
rate   the interest rate per period
nper   the total number of payments

The three functions that can be used with loans are:

=PMT (rate, nper, pv)
calculates the payment each period if the **rate, nper** and **pv** are known.
=RATE (nper, pmt, pv)
calculates the interest rate provided the **nper, pmt** and **pv** are known.
=PV (rate, nper, pmt)
calculates the loan value provided **rate, nper** and **pmt** are known.

Functions that are useful when dealing with investments are:

=FV (rate, nper, pmt)
calculates the final value of saving an amount (**pmt**) for a specific time (**nper**) at a given interest rate.
=NPV (rate, value1, value2…)
calculates the net present value of an investment using a comparison discount rate (**rate**) and a series of future income payments from the investment (positive values) and payments to the investment (negative payments). You can have up to 29 value arguments. Basically, if the NPV result is positive, the investment is worth doing.

Have a look at (and experiment with) these examples of how these functions can be used. You'll find other examples (and more information on these functions) in the Help system.

=PMT(RATE, NPER, PV)

You have decided to extend your house. Your architect estimates that it will cost £20,000. Your bank is prepared to give you a loan for this, at 10% interest per year, over 10 years. What is the monthly repayment on the loan? To work this, you can use the =PMT function. The arguments would be:

=PMT(10%/12, 10*12, 20000)
10%/12 is the monthly interest repayment
10*12 is the number of repayments you will make
20000 is the amount you will borrow

Your monthly repayments would be £264.30.

The full syntax of the **Pmt** function is:

=PMT(rate, nper, pv, fv, type)

FV is the future value of the loan (a cash balance) you want to have after all payments have been made. It is optional and if omitted, the **Pmt** function assumes a FV value of zero.

Type is also optional. It indicates **when** the payments are due. Type can either be:

Value	Explanation
0	Payments are due at the end of the period (default)
1	Payments are due at the beginning of the period

If the Type parameter is omitted, the **Pmt** function assumes a Type value of 0 – payments are due at the end of the period.

=RATE (nper, pmt, pv)

What is the interest rate of a four-year loan for £10,000 with a monthly payment (at the end of the month) of £390?

=RATE (4*12, -390, 10000)
4*12 is the number of repayments
-390 is the amount that you repay each month
10000 is the amount of the loan
The interest rate is 3%.

=PV (rate, nper, pmt)

You need to borrow some money to buy a car. You have worked out your finances, and have calculated that the most you can afford to pay back each month is £250. Your bank is willing to offer you a loan, over four years, at 5% interest. How much can you afford to borrow?

=PV(5%/12, 4*12, -250)
5%/12 is the interest rate per month
4*12 is the number of payments over the 4 years
-250 is the amount that you pay each month

The amount you can afford to borrow is £10,855.74.

=FV (rate, nper, pmt)

You inherit £10,000 that is deposited in a savings account that pays 7% annual interest. If you leave the interest in the account and deposit a further £1000 at the end of each subsequent year, what will the savings account be worth in 10 years' time?

=FV(7%, 10, -1000, -10000)
7% is the interest paid each year
10 is the number of payments
-1000 is the amount that you pay each year
-10000 is the initial amount deposited when you opened the account (the pv)

Your savings account will be worth £33,487.96.

=NPV (rate, value1, value2...)

You are considering investing £20,000 in a venture which will pay you an annual income of £7200, £8400 and £10,400 in the next three years. The current rate of interest is 7.5%. What is the NPV of your investment?

=NPV(7.5%, -20000, 7200, 8400, 10400)
7.5% is the interest rate
-20000 is the initial payment (negative value as you paid it in)
7200, 8400, 10400 are the amounts that you receive in the next three years (positive values as it is money you receive)

The NPV of your investment would be £2174.94.

6.6 Lookup functions

You can locate values in a table using the **HLOOKUP** (horizontal) or **VLOOKUP** (vertical) functions. Use **HLOOKUP** when your comparison values are located in the **first row** of the range that you are looking up (the *table array*). The format of the function is:

=HLOOKUP(Lookup value, table array, row number, Range_lookup)

You can identify the column using cell addresses or column labels.

	A	B	C	D	E	F
1	Country	Life Expectancy	Population (mills)			
2	France	76	96		HLOOKUP	
3	Gambia	44	0.18		=HLOOKUP("Population (millions)",A1:C10,8)	Population of Portugal
4	Germany	75	77.6		=HLOOKUP("Life Expectancy",A1:C10,6)	Life expectancy in Italy
5	Ireland	78	0.3			
6	Italy	75	57.1		VLOOKUP	
7	Mozambique	47	15.2		=VLOOKUP("Gambia",A1:C10,2)	Life expectancy in Gambia
8	Portugal	74	10.3		=VLOOKUP("Spain",A1:C10,3}	Population of Spain
9	Spain	77	39.1			
10	UK	76	57.1			
11						

LOOKUP formulas...

	E11	▼	f_x				
	A	B	C	D	E	F	G
1	Country	Life Expectancy	Population (mills)				
2	France	76	96		HLOOKUP		
3	Gambia	44	0.18		10.3	Population of Portugal	
4	Germany	75	77.6		75	Life expectancy in Italy	
5	Ireland	78	0.3				
6	Italy	75	57.1		VLOOKUP		
7	Mozambique	47	15.2		44	Life expectancy in Gambia	
8	Portugal	74	10.3		39.1	Population of Spain	
9	Spain	77	39.1				
10	UK	76	57.1				

... and their results

Author's insight

Sort the data you are *looking up* into ascending order based on the first row (HLOOKUP) or first column (VLOOKUP) of the range before you start.

LOOKUP functions compare your Lookup value with the values in the **first row** (HLOOKUP) or **column** (VLOOKUP) of the data identified by the table array (the cell range that you are looking up).

Once the nearest match (or exact match) is found it returns the corresponding value from the **row** (HLOOKUP) or **column** (VLOOKUP) specified from the range of cells looked up.

If you want an exact match (rather than the closest match) for the value you are looking up add FALSE to the Range_lookup field. Range_lookup is optional – if you omit a value it assumes you want the closest match to your Lookup value.

Use **VLOOKUP** when your comparison values are located in the **first column** of the range you are looking up.

   =VLOOKUP(Lookup value, table array, column number, Range_lookup)

You can identify the row using cell addresses or row labels.

IF AND LOOKUP

It is often possible to solve a problem in more than one way. When evaluating something with a view to returning a value you can often use either an IF (or nested IFs) – or a Lookup function.

You can nest up to 64 IFs – but things can become a bit confusing if you nest too many. A Lookup will often be easier to use if there are lots of possible outcomes.

For example (extending the example on page 109) you could use Excel to record student results, and assign a grade e.g. A+, A, A-, B+, B, B-,...E+, E, E-, F+, F, F- using nested IFs.

Alternatively, you could use a Lookup to achieve the same result – and it would probably be easier.

Consider the following example:

	A	B	C	D	E	F	G	H	I	J	K	L	M	N	O	P	Q	R	S	T	U	V	W
1	**END OF TERM EXAM RESULTS**						10	15	20	25	30	35	40	45	50	55	60	65	70	75	80	85	90	95
2							F-	F	F+	E-	E	E+	D-	D	D+	C-	C	C+	B-	B	B+	A-	A	A+
3	**Firstname**	**Surname**	**Mark awarded**	**Grade**																				
4	Ann	Allan	48	D																				
5	Andrew	Borthwick	52	D+																				
6	Peter	Jackson	91	A																				
7	Gill	McLaren	45	D																				
8	Alison	Smith	50	D+																				
9	Hector	Smith	68	C+																				
10	William	Smith	72	B-																				
11	David	Watson	59	C-																				
12	Pauline	Watson	65	C+																				
13	Marion	Williamson	49	D																				

The Grade column **could** be completed using a nested IF – similar to page 139 – for the **18 grades**.

Alternatively, by entering the grades onto the worksheet, in **ascending** order, and then naming the range (in this case F1:W2 is named Grade) a simple HLOOKUP gives the same result as a rather tricky nested IF. The table shows how the function is constructed:

Lookup value	Range to look up	Column to select data from	Optional – Range_lookup
=HLOOKUP(C4,	Grade	2	
Horizontally look for a value matching that in C4	In the **first row** of the range of cells named Grade If you use cell addresses to identify the lookup range, you should absolutely address them, e.g. $F$1:$W$2	Return the data in **row two** of that range	Leave blank, or enter True, if the closest match is **OK** – as in this example. If you are just interested in an *exact* match – enter **False**

6.7 Data tables

A data table is a range of values that can be substituted into a formula.

There are two types of data tables – one-variable (where one value in the formula is substituted) and two-variable (where two values in the formula are substituted).

ONE-VARIABLE DATA TABLE

In a one-variable data table, the values can be listed down a column or across a row.

In this example, we have a distance of 4000 miles to travel, and want to work out how long the journey will take. We can use a one-variable data table to show us how long it will take to travel the distance. The time taken depends on the speed at which we travel (the variable). The basic formula to calculate the time it takes will be Distance/Speed.

1 Enter the distance that you need to travel in a cell, e.g. B2.
2 Enter the variable data (the speeds that you could average each hour) either across one row or down one column, e.g. A5:A8.

Column-orientated table:
1 Type the formula (B2/E2) that refers to the input cell in the row above the first value and one cell to the right of the column of values, e.g. B4. Type any additional formulas to the right of the first formula.

	A	B	C	D	E
1	Column-orientated Data Table				
2	Distance	4000	miles	Speed (input cell)	40
3	Speed (input values) miles per hour	Hours taken			
4		100			
5	40	100			
6	50	80			
7	60	67			
8	70	57			

2 Select the range of cells that contain the formulas and values that you want to substitute – A4:B8.

3 On the **Data** tab, click **What-If Analysis** in the **Data Tools** group and select **Data Table** from the options.

4 Type the cell reference for the input cell in the Column input cell box – E2.

5 Click **OK**.

	E2 ▾	_fx_	40		
	A	B	C	D	E
1	**Column-orientated Data Table**				
2	Distance	4000	miles	Speed (input cell)	40
3	Speed (input values) miles per hour	Hours taken			
4		=B2/E2			
5	40	=TABLE(,E2)			
6	50	=TABLE(,E2)			
7	60	=TABLE(,E2)			
8	70	=TABLE(,E2)			
9					

Row-orientated table:

1 Type the formula in the column to the left of the first value and one cell below the row of values. Type any additional formulas below the first formula.

2 Select the range of cells that contain the formulas and values you want to substitute.

3 On the **Data** tab, click **What-If Analysis** in the **Data Tools** group and select **Data Table** from the options.

4 Type the cell reference for the input cell in the Row input cell box.

TWO-VARIABLE DATA TABLE

A two-variable input table is very similar, but with a row and a column input value. You could create a two-variable input table to calculate the 'times tables' from 1 to 12.

1 Enter the formula that refers to the two input cells in a cell on the worksheet (in B4 in this example).

2 Enter one list of input values in the same column, below the formula.

3 Enter the second list of input values in the same row, to the right of the formula.

4 Select the range of cells that contains the formula and both the row and column of values (B4:N16).

5 On the **Data** tab, click **What-If Analysis** in the **Data Tools** group and select **Data Table** from the options.

6 In the Row input cell box, enter the reference to the input cell for the input values in the row.

7 In the Column input cell box, enter the reference to the input cell for the input values in the column.

8 Click **OK**.

Go to one-variable and two-variable data tables in Help for more information.

	A	B	C	D	E	F	G	H	I	J	K	L	M	N
1	Table	1												
2	Number	1												
3							Table							
4		1	1	2	3	4	5	6	7	8	9	10	11	12
5		1	1	2	3	4	5	6	7	8	9	10	11	12
6		2	2	4	6	8	10	12	14	16	18	20	22	24
7		3	3	6	9	12	15	18	21	24	27	30	33	36
8		4	4	8	12	16	20	24	28	32	36	40	44	48
9		5	5	10	15	20	25	30	35	40	45	50	55	60
10		6	6	12	18	24	30	36	42	48	54	60	66	72
11		7	7	14	21	28	35	42	49	56	63	70	77	84
12		8	8	16	24	32	40	48	56	64	72	80	88	96
13		9	9	18	27	36	45	54	63	72	81	90	99	108
14		10	10	20	30	40	50	60	70	80	90	100	110	120
15		11	11	22	33	44	55	66	77	88	99	110	121	132
16		12	12	24	36	48	60	72	84	96	108	120	132	144
17														

The completed data table showing values...

The table shows cell contents:

	A	B	C	D	E	F	G
1	Table	1					
2	Number	1					
3							Ta
4		=B1*B2	1	2	3	4	5
5		1	=TABLE(B2,B1)	=TABLE(B2,B1)	=TABLE(B2,B1)	=TABLE(B2,B1)	=TABLE(B2,B1)
6		2	=TABLE(B2,B1)	=TABLE(B2,B1)	=TABLE(B2,B1)	=TABLE(B2,B1)	=TABLE(B2,B1)
7		3	=TABLE(B2,B1)	=TABLE(B2,B1)	=TABLE(B2,B1)	=TABLE(B2,B1)	=TABLE(B2,B1)
8		4	=TABLE(B2,B1)	=TABLE(B2,B1)	=TABLE(B2,B1)	=TABLE(B2,B1)	=TABLE(B2,B1)
9		5	=TABLE(B2,B1)	=TABLE(B2,B1)	=TABLE(B2,B1)	=TABLE(B2,B1)	=TABLE(B2,B1)
10		6	=TABLE(B2,B1)	=TABLE(B2,B1)	=TABLE(B2,B1)	=TABLE(B2,B1)	=TABLE(B2,B1)
11		7	=TABLE(B2,B1)	=TABLE(B2,B1)	=TABLE(B2,B1)	=TABLE(B2,B1)	=TABLE(B2,B1)
12		8	=TABLE(B2,B1)	=TABLE(B2,B1)	=TABLE(B2,B1)	=TABLE(B2,B1)	=TABLE(B2,B1)
13		9	=TABLE(B2,B1)	=TABLE(B2,B1)	=TABLE(B2,B1)	=TABLE(B2,B1)	=TABLE(B2,B1)
14		10	=TABLE(B2,B1)	=TABLE(B2,B1)	=TABLE(B2,B1)	=TABLE(B2,B1)	=TABLE(B2,B1)
15		11	=TABLE(B2,B1)	=TABLE(B2,B1)	=TABLE(B2,B1)	=TABLE(B2,B1)	=TABLE(B2,B1)
16		12	=TABLE(B2,B1)	=TABLE(B2,B1)	=TABLE(B2,B1)	=TABLE(B2,B1)	=TABLE(B2,B1)

... and showing formulas

Tips for using data tables

Set up a **base model** – the basic information, completed with a single set of data, just to demonstrate what you are doing.

Don't change the values in the **base model** – then you can always refer back to it.

Document the area around your data table clearly – so that it is obvious what it is doing.

And remember:

You can use data tables to change up to **two** variables only.

You can create as many one-variable or two-variable data tables as you like in a workbook.

6.8 Goal Seek

Another useful What-If function is Goal Seek. This allows you to specify the goal you are seeking, and get Excel to work out the value of a given source cell to enable you to reach your goal. The cell whose value you are changing – in our example the Payment value – must contain a formula.

Let's say you had decided to purchase a property, and you had worked out that you could afford to pay £750 per month in a mortgage. You have decided on a fixed rate mortgage, and the interest rate is 3%. You want to know how much you can borrow. Excel can help you work this out. Enter the data that you know into a worksheet (the Loan Amount is the unknown in this example, so enter any value initially). The Payment cell contains the formula =PMT(B2/12,B3,B1) – this will be the cell that we want to change during the Goal Seek.

	A	B	C	D	E
	B4		f_x =PMT(B2/12,B3,B1)		
1	Loan Amount	£ 100,000.00	amount borrowed		
2	Interest Rate	3%	fixed rate		
3	Period	180	payments over 15 years		
4	Payment	-£690.58	monthly payment		

We want to work out the Loan value, by setting the Payment cell value to £750.

1 On the **Data** tab, click **What-If Analysis** in the **Data Tools** group and select **Goal Seek...** from the options.

2 In the **Goal Seek** dialog box, set the conditions. Here we want to set the payment in B4 to –750 (minus because we are paying out), by changing the loan amount in cell B1.

3 Click **OK**.

4 At the **Goal Seek Solution** dialog box, your setting will be confirmed, and you will see the result on your worksheet – £108,604.10.

5 Click **OK** to close the dialog box and update the worksheet.

You might decide that this is not enough to purchase a property in your chosen area, and your sister offers to join forces with you so that you can both get onto the property ladder. Between you, you can afford to payback £1400 per month. If you check it out you should find that you can afford to borrow £202,727.66 between you.

6.9 Scenarios

A scenario is a named set of values that can be applied to a set of selected cells in your workbook. They are used when you want to set up a model where you can quickly substitute the various inputs so that you can compare the solutions. They are useful in 'What-If' situations, where you can set up several named inputs and apply them to you worksheet to help identify best and worst cases.

Let's say you wanted to perform some calculations to work out the monthly repayments that you would have to make on a loan. You are considering three options.

	Amount of loan	Interest rate	Payback period
Option 1	£20,000	7%	5 years
Option 2	£25,000	7%	8 years
Option 3	£30,000	10%	12 years

You could set up each option as a scenario.

1 Set up your worksheet to show the Option 1 payments and input the formula required.

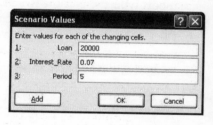

	B7	▼	fx	=PMT(Interest_Rate/12,Period*12,Loan)

	A	B	C	D	E
1	**Loan repayment calculations**				
2					
3	Loan	£20,000.00			
4	Interest Rate	7%	per annum		
5	Period	5	years		
6					
7	Payment	-£396.02			
8					

2   On the **Data** tab, click **What-If Analysis** in the **Data Tools** group and select **Scenario Manager** from the options.

3   At the **Scenario Manager** dialog box click **Add...**

4   Give the scenario a name, e.g. Option 1.

5   Specify the cells that will change when you show the various scenarios, e.g. B3:B5 and click **OK**.

6   Type the values in for Option 1 and click **Add**.

7   Repeat steps 4–6 for Option 2 and 3.

8   Click **OK**.

The scenarios will be listed in the **Scenario Manager** dialog box. If a scenario is wrong or no longer required, you can edit or delete it from this dialog box.

To see the repayment options, select an option and click **Show** – the values on your worksheet will be substituted by those in the scenario.

When you show each scenario in turn, you can see the outcome of applying that scenario only. If you wish to see the outcomes of all the scenarios at once (which makes it easier to compare them) you must create a scenario summary.

To create a scenario summary:
1 On the **Data** tab, click **What-If Analysis** in the **Data Tools** group and select **Scenario Manager...**
2 At the **Scenario Manager** dialog box click **Summary...**
3 Choose **Scenario summary** as the report type and edit the **Result cells:** field if necessary.
4 Click **OK**.

A new sheet will be created showing the summary report.

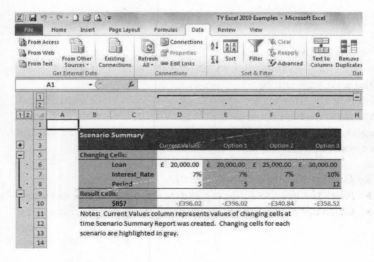

6.10 PivotTable

There may be times when you want to create a report that summarizes the data held in a worksheet. You might want to perform some calculations on the summarized data, or filter it to display specific data from the list. PivotTables can be used in this situation. They are interactive tables that allow you to summarize large amounts of data.

A PivotTable has four areas – page, column, row and data. The page, column and row areas show the data that you have added to the PivotTable – they act as labels for the data that you are summarizing. They are also used to filter the data that you add.

The data area is where the summary result calculations are performed and displayed. Each item in the data area must have a function associated with it – Sum, Average, Count, etc.

PAGE		COLUMN	
	ROW	DATA	

You don't have to have an item in the page, column or row area, but you must have something in the data area (you have to be summarizing something!).

In this example we've used Excel to record details of customer orders. We then go on to summarize this data using a PivotTable. We want to be able to:

▶ *Display the order data by town.*
▶ *Filter the data to show the order data from each customer.*
▶ *Calculate totals for the number of each item purchased.*

M24   fx

	A	B	C	D	E	F	G
1			**Gerry's Garden Centre**				
2							
3	**Order Summary for**		**December**				
4							
5	**Order ID**	**Date**	**Customer**	**Town**	**Roses**	**Lilies**	**Carnations**
6	FF100	01/01/2009	Fabby Flowers	Edinburgh	30	10	20
7	GT001	03/12/2009	Golden Tulip	Dalkeith	20	20	40
8	AF001	03/12/2009	Amy's Flowers	Edinburgh	50	60	80
9	FF101	04/12/2009	Fabby Flowers	Edinburgh	22	10	50
10	AF002	04/12/2009	Amy's Flowers	Edinburgh	60	30	20
11	GT002	06/12/2009	Golden Tulip	Dalkeith	16	22	30
12	BB001	06/12/2009	Best Blooms	Dalkeith	100	20	30
13	GT003	07/12/2009	Golden Tulip	Dalkeith	20	18	30
14	AF003	07/12/2009	Amy's Flowers	Edinburgh	60	50	90
15	FF102	08/12/2009	Fabby Flowers	Edinburgh	16	20	30
16	GT004	08/12/2009	Golden Tulip	Dalkeith	20	24	30
17	FF103	10/12/2009	Fabby Flowers	Edinburgh	18	22	50
18	BB002	10/12/2009	Best Blooms	Dalkeith	20	20	20
19	GT005	11/12/2009	Golden Tulip	Dalkeith	14	20	70
20	GT006	12/12/2009	Golden Tulip	Dalkeith	14	16	60
21	FF104	15/12/2009	Fabby Flowers	Edinburgh	16	20	80
22	BB003	15/12/2009	Best Blooms	Dalkeith	30	50	70
23	GT006	16/12/2009	Golden Tulip	Dalkeith	20	30	50

To create a PivotTable:

1 Click anywhere inside the list of data for which you want to create a PivotTable.
2 On the **Insert** tab, click the **PivotTable** command button in the **Tables** group.
3 Choose the **Select a table or range** option, check the cell range and edit if necessary.
4 Specify where you want the PivotTable displayed.
5 Click **OK**.

PivotTable

The PivotTable is created, and the PivotTable Tools are displayed in the Ribbon, with an **Options** tab and a **Design** tab.

To layout your data:

1 Select the fields that you want to appear in the PivotTable.

2 Drag and drop the fields from one report area to another to see how this affects the layout of your chart.

■ If you click outside the **PivotTable** area, the **PivotTable Tools** and the **Field List** pane disappear – just click anywhere within the PivotTable to display them again.

Show/Hide

Once you have laid out your PivotTable, experiment with the **Show** buttons to see their effect.

Try moving the fields from one area to another to see the effect it has on your PivotTable, e.g. drag the Town into the **Report Filter** area.

PivotTable Actions and Properties

■ To clear your PivotTable (so you can start again!) – click the **Clear** button in the **PivotTable Actions** group and then choose **Clear All**.

■ To name your PivotTable, edit the default name in the **PivotTable Properties**.

■ To move your PivotTable, click the **Move PivotTable** button in the **PivotTable Actions** group. You can move it to a new worksheet, or to another location in the existing sheet.

Data

■ When the source data is updated, click the **Refresh** button in the **Data** group to update the data in your PivotTable.

■ If you wish to change or edit the data source, use the **Change Data Source** button to open a dialog box where you can adjust the source range.

To change the design of your PivotTable:

■ Display the **Design** tab in the **PivotTable** tools.

Experiment with the **Layout, PivotTable Style Options** and **PivotTable Styles** to see what options are available to you.

6.11 Consolidating data

Consolidation is used to combine values from multiple ranges into one new range, while processing the values using an Excel function, e.g. Sum, Count, Average, Minimum.

There are various ways of consolidating your data, but the most commonly used options are discussed here.

	B4		f_x		
	A	B	C	D	E
1	**Branch Sales Figures**				
2	**January - April**				
3		**Tyres**	**Exhausts**	**Accessories**	**Total**
4	**Aberdeen**				£ -
5	**Dunfermline**				£ -
6	**Dundee**				£ -
7	**Edinburgh**				£ -
8	**Glasgow**				£ -
9	**Inverness**				£ -
10	**Perth**				£ -
11	**Total**	£ -	£ -	£ -	
12					

CONSOLIDATE BY POSITION

You could use this method if the source data and the destination data are laid out in the same way. This example consolidates data from four separate worksheets – January, February, March and April. These sheets contain sales data for company branches. The data for each month has the same layout, as has the worksheet being used to consolidate the data.

1 Select the range of cells that the source data will be consolidated into.
2 Click the **Consolidate** button in the **Data Tools** group on the **Data** tab.

3 Select the function from the **Function** list.

4 Enter the first cell range into the **Reference** field.

5 Click **Add**.

6 Repeat steps 4 and 5 for each range you wish to add.

7 Select the **Create links to source data** checkbox if you want the consolidated data to be updated any time the source data changes.

8 Click **OK**.

■ If the **Create links** checkbox is selected, the outline pane is open so you can expand and collapse the level of detail displayed as required.

		A	B	C	D	E
	1			**Branch Sales Figures**		
	2			**January - April**		
	3		**Tyres**	**Exhausts**	**Accessories**	**Total**
+	8	Aberdeen	£ 11,100.00	£ 11,800.00	£ 9,900.00	£32,800.00
+	13	Dunfermline	£ 12,900.00	£ 10,400.00	£ 15,500.00	£38,800.00
+	18	Dundee	£ 13,000.00	£ 10,600.00	£ 11,200.00	£34,800.00
+	23	Edinburgh	£ 20,600.00	£ 19,600.00	£ 21,000.00	£61,200.00
+	28	Glasgow	£ 20,500.00	£ 21,000.00	£ 18,500.00	£60,000.00
+	33	Inverness	£ 13,500.00	£ 13,000.00	£ 13,500.00	£40,000.00
+	38	Perth	£ 12,700.00	£ 9,200.00	£ 18,500.00	£40,400.00
	39	Total	£ 197,500.00	£ 179,400.00	£ 206,300.00	
	40					

CONSOLIDATE BY FORMULA

You could also consolidate your data by using a formula that references cells in different worksheets. The data may be in different cells on each sheet, or in the same cell in each sheet.

It is not necessary to have the consolidated data presented using the same layout as the source data.

To enter the formula or function:

1 Select the cell that will contain the formula or function.

2 Type in the formula or function (or use **Insert Function**).

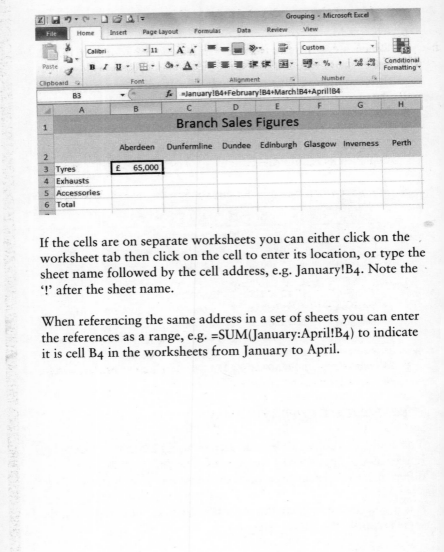

If the cells are on separate worksheets you can either click on the worksheet tab then click on the cell to enter its location, or type the sheet name followed by the cell address, e.g. January!B4. Note the '!' after the sheet name.

When referencing the same address in a set of sheets you can enter the references as a range, e.g. =SUM(January:April!B4) to indicate it is cell B4 in the worksheets from January to April.

THINGS TO REMEMBER

1 *The key Logical functions are IF, AND, OR. Logic and math are combined in the functions COUNTIF and SUMIF.*

2 *There are functions for manipulating text, including CONCATENATE, UPPER, LOWER, and PROPER.*

3 *The Date functions, such as TODAY, NOW, DAY, MONTH and YEAR use the computer's clock and calendar.*

4 *Financial functions that are used when dealing with loans and investments.*

5 *You can pull matching data from a list using the Lookup functions.*

6 *There are a set of tool for What-If Analysis tools – data tables, Goal Seek and scenarios.*

7 *Pivot Tables offer a different way to view and analyse data.*

8 *Where sheets have matching layouts, you can consolidate data in a summary sheet.*

TEST

	A	B	C	D	E
1	Today's date	19 August 2009			
2	**Stock Clearance Sale**				
3	Item	No in stock	Put in sale?	Rec Retail Price	Sale Price
4	Desks	10	Yes	£ 750.00	£ 375.00
5	Tables	6	No	£ 950.00	£ 950.00
6	Chairs	15	Yes	£ 225.00	£ 112.50
7	Sofas	9	No	£ 925.00	£ 925.00
8					
9	**Number of items in sale**		25		
10					
11	**Summary of stock held**		10 Desks @ £750 (Rec Retail Price)		
12			6 Tables @ £950 (Rec Retail Price)		
13			15 Chairs @ £225 (Rec Retail Price)		
14			9 Sofas @ £925 (Rec Retail Price)		

1 *What function is used in B1 to display today's date (this function will be volatile and change automatically)?*

2 *If there are 10 or more items in stock, the item will go in the sale. What function is in column C to display Yes next to items for the sale, and No next to items that will not go in the sale?*

3 *What function has been used in column E to calculate the sale price of items that will go in the sale?*

4 *What function has been used in C9 to give the total number of items that will be in the sale?*

5 *What function has been used in C11 – copied through C12:C14 – to display the summary of stock held?*

6 *Give one example of a financial function used for loan calculations, and one example used for investment calculations.*

7 A **Lookup** *function is sometimes used as an alternative to another commonly used function discussed in this chapter. What is it?*

8 *Give three examples of functions used in What-If type functions (other than the IF function).*

9 *Page, Row, Column and Data areas are found in what kind of table?*

10 *You can consolidate data in two ways – what are they?*

7

Charting and drawing

In this chapter you will learn:
- *how to produce charts from your data*
- *about printing charts*
- *how to add special effects to your charts*
- *about Shapes*

7.1 Preparing your data

Excel can create charts – bar graphs, line graphs, pie charts, scatter diagrams, etc. – from the data in your worksheet.

You can create your chart on the same worksheet as the data on which the chart is built (an embedded chart), or on a separate chart sheet.

> ▶ *Ideally the data should be in adjacent cells.*
> ▶ *If there are blank rows or columns within the data to be charted, remove these before you try to chart it.*

To chart data that is not in adjacent cells:
1 Select the first group of cells you want to chart.
2 Hold down [Ctrl] while you click and drag over the other groups you want to include in your chart.

When the non-adjacent cells are selected, the areas must be able to combine to form a rectangle.

Depending on the type of data you are charting, you must ensure that the data is laid out correctly on your worksheet if you hope to chart it successfully. See 'How to arrange data for specific chart types' in 'Create a chart' in the online Help.

7.2 Creating a chart

To create a chart:

1 Select the cells you want to create a chart from.
2 On the **Insert** tab, in the **Charts** group, click the **Chart Type** button, then click on the subtype you want to use.

Or

3 Click **All Chart Types** at the bottom of the list to display the **Create Chart** dialog box, where all chart types and subtypes are located. Select the chart type and click **OK**.

The resulting chart is embedded within the worksheet that contains the source data.

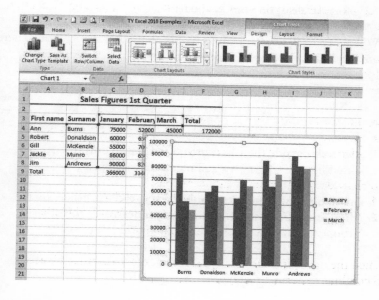

MOVE, RESIZE AND DELETE CHARTS

If you want to move, resize or delete a chart that is an object on a worksheet, you must select the chart first.

To move the chart:
1 Select the chart.
2 Point to the edge of the chart – the mouse pointer changes to a four-headed arrow when you are in the correct place.
3 Drag and drop the chart in its new location.

To resize the chart:
1 Select the chart.
2 Point to one of the handles in the corner or along the edge of the chart – the mouse pointer changes to a two-headed arrow when you are in the correct place.
3 Click and drag to resize the chart.

To delete the chart:
1 Select the chart.
2 Press [**Delete**] on your keyboard.

When a chart is selected, **Chart Tools** appear on the Ribbon. There are three tabs – **Design, Layout** and **Format**.

If you click outside the Chart area, the **Chart Tools** disappear. Click within the Chart area again and they reappear.

If you don't want your chart embedded in the worksheet that contains its source data, you can easily move it.

To move a chart to a new location:
1 Select the **Design** tab from the **Chart Tools**.
2 Click the **Move Chart** button in the **Location** group.
3 Select the location.
4 Click **OK**.

If your chart doesn't look the way you expected, and you think a different chart type would be better, you can change the type at any time.

To change the chart type:
1 Click the **Change Chart Type** button in the **Type** group on the **Design** tab.
2 Select the type and subtype.
3 Click **OK**.

7.3 Adjusting your source data

You can edit the data series for a chart by:

- ▶ *Editing the range of source data for the whole chart.*
- ▶ *Selecting a new range of source data for the whole chart.*
- ▶ *Editing the ranges that affect the legend entries (series).*
- ▶ *Editing the ranges that affect the horizontal axis labels (categories).*
- ▶ *Rearranging the legend entries.*
- ▶ *Switching the legend entries and horizontal axis labels.*

Display the **Select Data Source** dialog box to change the cell references of the source data.

  1 Click the **Select Data** button in the **Data** group.

To edit the range of chart data, or specify a new range:

  2 Amend the Chart Data Range.

To amend the legend entries:

  3 Select the entry.
  4 Click **Edit**.

5 At the **Select Data Source** dialog box amend the cell
   address that identifies the Series name and/or values and
   click **OK**.
6 If you wish to rearrange the series, select the item you wish to
   move and click the **Move up** and **Move down** buttons in the
   Select Data Source dialog box.

You can also **Add** new legend entries and **Remove** existing ones
from this dialog box (but this is also done automatically if you
adjust the Chart Data Range field).

To amend the horizontal axis labels (categories):
7 Click the **Edit** button and adjust the range of source cells in
   the **Axis Labels** dialog box.
8 Click **OK**.

To switch the data:
■ Click the **Switch Row/Column** button in the **Data** group on
   the **Design** tab.
Or
■ Click **Switch Row/Column** in the **Select Data Source**
   dialog box.

7.4 Chart styles and layouts

Excel has a variety of chart styles and layouts that you can use to quickly adjust and format your chart.

CHART STYLE

The chart styles give you access to a wide range of carefully colour-coordinated options that can be applied to your chart.

To change the chart style:
1 Select your chart.
2 Scroll through the **Chart Style** options on the **Design** tab of the Chart Tools.

Or

■ Click the **More** button at the bottom right of the **Chart Style** group to display the chart styles gallery.
3 Select the one you want to use.

CHART LAYOUT

The layout affects the inclusion and positioning of objects like the chart heading, legend, data table, axis labels, etc.

The quickest way to include/exclude objects from your chart is to use one of the predefined chart layouts.

1 Select your chart.
2 Scroll through the **Chart Layout** options on the **Design** tab of the Chart tools.

Or

■ Click the **More** button on the **Chart Layout** group to display the layout gallery.
3 Select one.

If you wish, you can customize any object within your chart – the chart title, axis titles, legend.

To delete a chart object:
1 Right-click on it.
2 Select **Delete** from the menu.

To format a chart object:
1 Right-click on the object.
2 Left-click on the **Format Chart Area.../Title.../Data Series...** option (depending on what you right-clicked on).
3 Explore the dialog box, selecting the options required.
4 Click **OK**.

CHART TITLES AND AXIS LABELS

These areas are text boxes, and initially contain default text – chart title in the title area and axis title along each axis.

To replace the default text:
1 Click once on the label to select it.
2 Click on it a second time to place the insertion point in it.
3 Delete the default text.
4 Type in your label.
5 Click outside the title or label area – anywhere on the chart.

Author's insight

You can also complete a label by selecting the label, typing the label text into the Formula bar and then pressing [**Enter**].

CHART LAYOUT OPTIONS

You can switch individual objects on and off using the buttons in the Labels, Axes and Background groups of the Layout tab, or reposition objects that have been displayed by applying one of the standard layouts.

- ▶ The **Labels** group includes the Chart Headings, Axis Titles, Legend, Data Labels and Data Table.
- ▶ The **Axes** group includes the Axes and the Gridlines.
- ▶ The **Background** group includes the Plot Area (2-D charts), Chart Wall, Chart Floor and 3D View (3-D charts).

To display an object or change its position:
1 Click the object's button.
2 Select the position required.

To remove an object:
1 Click the object's button.
2 Select **None**.

To adjust the format of an object:
1 Click the object's button.
2 Select **More Options...** and explore the dialog box.
3 Select the options and click **OK**.

Some objects have many more options than others. Walls, floors and plot areas have fill colours and fill effects. Lines have styles, colours and widths. The best idea is to explore and experiment – some options will appeal to you, others will not. But don't overdo things! The purpose of your chart will be to clearly and effectively present your data – not demonstrate every Excel chart formatting option!

7.5 More formatting options

The Format tab offers even more formatting options.

The Current Selection group gives you:

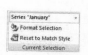

- ► **Format Selection** *which opens the Format dialog box for the object selected.*
- ► **Reset to Match Style** – *useful if you have been experimenting and want to get back to the original formatting.*

The Shape Styles group gives access to formatting options that affect the fill, outline and shape of the current selection.

Select the options required from the buttons in the group, or click the Format Shape dialog launcher in the bottom right corner of the group to open the dialog box, giving access to all the options for the selected object.

7.6 Default chart

The default chart in Excel is a 2-D column chart.

To quickly produce the default chart:
1 Select the data you wish to chart.
2 Press [F11].

The chart will be displayed in a separate chart sheet, and you can use the Chart Tools to format it as you wish.

If you don't use 2-D column charts very often, you can change the default chart type.

To change the default chart type:

1 Display the **Insert Chart** or **Change Chart Type** dialog box.
2 Select the chart type and subtype to set as the default.
3 Click the **Set as Default Chart** button.
4 Click **Cancel** to exit the dialog box without creating a chart, or **OK** to create a chart.

CHART TEMPLATES

If you have created a chart layout that you wish to base other charts on you can save it as a template. This can save you a lot of time when creating charts in the future.

To create a chart template:

1 Create a chart, and format it as you wish – apply the chart style required, add the labels required, etc.
2 On the **Chart Tools** tab, **Design** group, click **Save as template**.
3 Give your template a name.
4 Click **OK**.

To create a chart using your template:
1 Select the data on which to base your chart.
2 Click a chart type on the Insert tab and choose **All Chart Types** at the bottom of the drop-down list.
3 Select **Templates** in the **Insert Chart** dialog box.
4 Choose your template and click **OK**.

7.7 Special effects

One of the best ways to find out about the charting capabilities is to experiment. However, here are some tips and pointers if you want to get that little bit more from your charts!

VALUE AXIS SCALE

By default, the value axis starts at o. If you don't have any small values to plot, e.g. if they all are 100,000 and over, this results in a large dead area at the bottom of your chart. To get rid of this, set an appropriate minimum value for the axis.

1 Right-click on the value axis and choose **Format Axis**.
2 In the **Axis Options**, set the minimum value for the axis.
3 Click **Close**.

Format Axis

Axis Options	**Axis Options**
Number	Minimum: ○ Auto ● Fixed `30000`
Fill	Maximum: ● Auto ○ Fixed `100000.0`
Line Color	Major unit: ● Auto ○ Fixed `10000.0`
Line Style	Minor unit: ● Auto ○ Fixed `2000.0`
Shadow	☐ Values in reverse order
Glow and Soft Edges	☐ Logarithmic scale Base: `10`
3-D Format	Display units: `None` ▾
Alignment	☐ Show display units label on chart

Major tick mark type: `Outside` ▾

Minor tick mark type: `None` ▾

Axis labels: `Next to Axis` ▾

Horizontal axis crosses:
- ● Automatic
- ○ Axis value: `0.0`
- ○ Maximum axis value

[Close]

DISPLAY UNITS

This is another axis formatting option that is useful for large numbers on the value axis. You can opt to show the units rounded to hundreds, thousands, tens of thousands, hundreds of thousands, millions, tens of millions, hundreds of millions, billions or trillions!

Explore the other options in this dialog box to see if they would improve your charts.

OVERLAPS AND GAP WIDTHS

The spacing between each bar or column on a chart is called the
overlap. The space between each group of bars or columns is the
gap width. You can adjust these settings from the Format Data
Series dialog box.

1 Right-click on any data series.
2 Choose **Format Data Series...** from the pop-up menu.
3 Set the **Overlap** and/or **Gap** settings as required.
4 Click **Close**.

PICTURE OR TEXTURE FILL

The Fill options for a data series include Picture or Texture Fill.
The Picture can be from a file, Clipboard or ClipArt.

1 In the **Fill** options, select **Picture** or **Texture fill**.

2 Click:
> **File...** to use a picture file.
> **Clipboard** to paste in an image you have copied to the
> Clipboard.
> **ClipArt...** to search for a suitable piece of ClipArt.

3 Locate your file/ClipArt image and insert it.
4 Close the dialog box.

Author's insight

Pictographs (created using pictures to represent the data in a series) can be very effective in some situations.

When using a picture, experiment with the Stretch, Stack, Stack and Scale options in the Fill category of the Format Data Series dialog box to create the desired effect.

COMBINED CHARTS

You can customize charts further by combining some chart types (you can't combine all types – experiment with them).

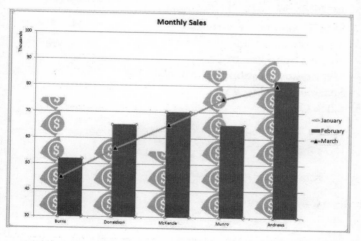

To combine a column chart with a line chart:
1 Display a column chart in 2-D.
2 Select the series that you wish to display as a line.
3 Click **Change Chart Type** on the **Design** tab.
4 Choose **Line**, then the subtype from the **Chart type** list.
5 Close the dialog box.
6 Format the line as you wish.

SPARKLINES

A Sparkline is a mini chart that is used to show trends in your data. The Sparkline is displayed in the background of a cell, and is most effective if it is next to, or very close, to the data it represents.

They are very easy to produce, and can help a reader see how the data has developed visually – which can be easier to interpret that just reading the data on a datasheet.

To create a Sparkline:
1 Display the **Insert** tab in the Ribbon.
2 Select the Sparkline layout required – **Line, Column** or **Win/Loss**.
3 Select the data range that you want to create a Sparkline from.
4 Identify the location that you want the Sparkline displayed in.
5 Click **OK**.

	A	B	C	D	E	F	G
1	Sales Figures 1st Quarter						
2							
3	First name	Surname	January	February	March	Total	
4	Ann	Burns	75000	25000	45000	145000	
5	Robert	Donaldson	60000	65000	56000	181000	
6	Gill	McKenzie	55000	100000	65000	220000	
7	Jackie	Munro	86000	65000	75000	226000	
8	Jim	Andrews	90000	55000	80000	225000	
9	Total		366000	310000	321000	997000	
10							

Once created, you can use the Sparkline Tools to edit, format or clear the Sparklines as required.

7.8 Printing your chart

You can print your chart with or without the data on which it is based. If it is an object in a worksheet you have several print options.

To print the chart and all of the data on the worksheet:
- Print the worksheet as normal (i.e. without selecting the chart).

To get a printout of the chart only:
- Select the chart on the worksheet, then print.

To print the chart, plus its data, but no other data:
1 Select the chart.
2 Choose a layout that displays the data table.
3 Print out with the chart selected.

To print a chart that is on a separate chart sheet:

1 Select the chart sheet.
- If you want to print out the data, choose a layout with a data table.
2 Print as usual.

Author's insight

You can adjust the Page Setup options on the Page Layout tab to get the orientation, margins and paper size required.

You can also click the Dialog Box launcher to display even more Page Setup options in the dialog box.

However, you cannot automatically centre a chart horizontally or vertically on the page (Margins tab, Page Setup dialog box).

7.9 Shapes buttons

Use the Shapes buttons to add effects to your charts and data, e.g. you could draw an arrow, with a message attached, pointing to an object within your chart.

- The Shapes are on the Insert tab on the Ribbon (in the Illustrations group).

To draw a shape:

1 Click **Shapes** on the **Insert** tab.   Shapes ▾
2 Select the shape required.
3 Click and drag on your worksheet to draw the shape.

Or

- To create a default-sized shape, click the shape required, then just click on your worksheet.

DRAWING TOOLS

When you select a drawing shape, the Drawing Tools appear in the Ribbon. If no shape is selected, the Drawing Tools disappear again.

You can use the buttons on the Format tab to format the shapes that you draw. To format your object in any way, you must select it first. Deselect it when you have finished.

To move or resize your shape:
- Click and drag within the object to move it.
- Click and drag a handle to resize the object.

If your shape must be a specific size, you can use the buttons in the Size group to set the size required.

To delete a shape:
- Press [**Delete**].

SHAPE STYLES

Use the Shape Styles buttons to select a different formatting style for your shape.

- ▶ **Shape Fill** *gives access to all the fill options available for an object, e.g. colour, picture, gradient or texture.*
- ▶ **Shape Outline** *gives access to the line formatting options for the outline, e.g. colour, weight, dashes and arrows.*
- ▶ **Shape Effects** *gives access to a range of preset and fully customizable 3-D and shadow effects for your shape.*

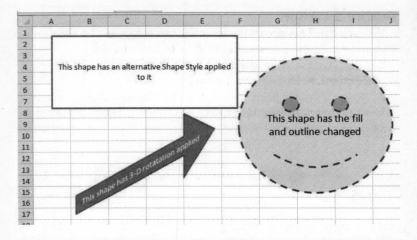

This shape has an alternative Shape Style applied to it

This shape has the fill and outline changed

This shape has 3-D rotatation applied

ADDING TEXT

To add text to a shape:
1. Right-click on the shape.
2. Select **Edit Text**.
3. Enter the text (or edit existing text).

If you wish to add free text to a worksheet or chart (not within
a shape or cell or as a chart object), you can use a text box. A text
box can be positioned anywhere on a worksheet or chart.

To insert a text box:

1 Click the **Text box** button on the **Insert** tab, in the **Text** group.

Or

- Click the **Text box** button in the **Insert Shapes** group on the **Format tab** of the Drawing tools.

2 Drag on your worksheet or chart to draw a rectangle where you want your text box to be.

3 Type in your text.

4 Click outside your text box.

A text box can be resized, moved, formatted or deleted like any other shape.

7.10 Some more options

You can create some interesting effects using shapes, particularly if you layer and group them, or rotate or flip them.

BRING FORWARD, SEND BACKWARD

When you draw your shapes, they are placed in layers on your worksheet. The first shape is on the lowest layer, the next one is on a layer above, the third shape on another layer above that, and so on.

If you move your shapes so that they overlap each other a little you will see this layering effect.

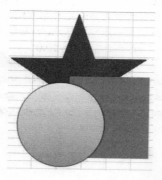

You can move a shape from one layer to another using the Bring Forward/Send Backward commands. These are located in the Arrange group on the Format tab of the Drawing tools.

BRING TO FRONT

Click the arrow beside the **Bring to Front** button to display the options:

▶ **Bring Forward** *moves a shape forward one layer at a time.*
▶ **Bring to Front** *moves the shape to the top.*

SEND TO BACK

Click the arrow beside the **Send to Back** button to display the options:

▶ **Send Backwards** *moves a shape back one layer at a time.*
▶ **Send to Back** *moves the shape to the bottom of the pile.*

The same shapes after resizing and reordering using the Bring to Front/Send to Back options.

GROUPING

If you create an image by layering several shapes, you will find it easier to manage the final image if you group the shapes together. Once the shapes are grouped they can be moved and resized as one object. You can always ungroup the objects again if you wish to edit each shape individually again.

To group shapes:

1 Select the shapes – select the first shape, then hold down [**Shift**] and click on each of the other shapes.

2 Click the **Group** button in the **Arrange** group and then click **Group** in the options.

The shapes are grouped together into one object and can then be resized, moved or deleted as one. If you need to work on an individual shape again, you must ungroup the object again.

To ungroup your shapes:

1 Select the grouped shape.

2 Click the **Group** button and select **Ungroup** from the list.

3 Edit the shapes as necessary.

To regroup the shapes that have been ungrouped:

1 Click the drop-down arrow to the right of the Group tool.

2 Choose **Regroup**.

SELECTION AND VISIBILITY PANE

As an alternative to using the Select, Bring Forward/Send Backward commands, you could use the Selection and Visibility pane.

To switch the pane off and on:

■ Click the **Selection Pane** button in the **Arrange** group.

To select a shape using the pane:

■ Click on the shape name in the list.

SHOW/HIDE SHAPE

To show or hide an individual shape:

■ Click the eye icon to the right of the shape name.

To show or hide all shapes on a sheet:

■ Click the **Show All** or **Hide All** buttons at the bottom of the pane.

To change the layer each shape
is on:

1 Select the shape.
2 Use the **Re-order** buttons at
the bottom of the pane.

To delete a shape:
1 Select it in the pane.
2 Press [**Delete**].

Show/Hide shape

Author's insight

You can align shapes with each other using the Align options
in the Arrange group on the Drawing Tools, Format tab.

Hold down [**Shift**] and click on each shape you want aligned,
and then choose the alignment required from the Align
options.

ROTATE AND FLIP

Shapes can be rotated left or right 90°, or freely through any angle,
or flipped horizontally or vertically.

To rotate a shape:
1 Select the shape.
2 Choose the rotate option from the **Rotate**
button in the **Arrange** group.

THINGS TO REMEMBER

1 *Excel has some powerful charting and drawing options available.*

2 *If data is organized into a table, it is easier to create a chart from it, but scattered data can be charted.*

3 *You can quickly create a chart using the default setting using the Ribbon tools.*

4 *If necessary you can adjust the data range of a chart.*

5 *There are many chart styles and layout and formatting options.*

6 *Sparklines can chart details with in charts.*

7 *Charts can be printed with or without their source data.*

8 *You can set your default chart styles.*

9 *Text, lines and shapes can be added to charts.*

TEST

1 *When selecting data to create a chart, the overall shape of the selection should be a:*
   a *Diamond*
   b *Circle*
   c *Rectangle.*

2 *To select non-adjacent cells for charting, hold down:*
   a *Shift*
   b *Ctrl*
   c *Alt*
   d *AltGr.*

3 *To create a default chart quickly, select the range of cells you wish to chart and then press:*
   a *[F1]*
   b *[F10]*
   c *[F11]*
   d *[F5].*

4 *Give three examples of chart types.*

5 *Explain what the terms 'overlap' and 'gap' mean.*

6 *How can you print a chart, without printing the data that the chart is based on?*

7 *How can you create a perfect square using a shape?*

8 *What effect does the Group, Ungroup and Regroup options have?*

9 *The Selection and Visibility pane list the shapes on your worksheet. There is an eye icon to the right of each shape. What is the eye used for?*

10 *What effect do rotate and flip options have?*

8

....

Styles and templates

In this chapter you will learn:
- *how to use, create and edit styles*
- *about workbook, worksheet and chart templates*

8.1 Cell styles

We looked at using standard Excel cell styles to format worksheets in Chapter 3. We will look at the options available to you when creating and working with your own styles here.

....

Author's insight

The main advantages of using styles are:

A consistent look to your worksheets and workbooks – within and across files.

Speed – they can speed up formatting tasks considerably.

....

To create your own style, either:
1 Format a cell with the attributes you want to add to a style, e.g. font size, colour, cell colour.
2 Select the cell and click **Cell Styles**, then **New Cell Style...**
3 Give your style a name.
4 Ensure that all the checkboxes required are selected (so that the style picks up the formats for the style from the selected cell).
5 Click **OK**.

Your style will now appear in the Cell list, so you can apply it to any other cells as required.

Or

1 Select any cell and click **Cell Styles**, then **New Cell Style...**
2 Give your style a name.
3 Ensure that all the checkboxes are cleared (unless the cell has an attribute that you wish to include in the style).
4 Click **Format** and format as required using the dialog box.
5 Click **OK**.

To rename or edit a style:

1 Click **Cell Styles** to display the styles.
2 Right-click on the style you wish to change.
3 Click **Modify...**
4 Make your changes – change the name or any of the formatting options.
5 Click **OK**.

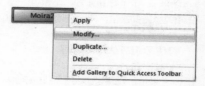

TABLE STYLES

Table styles can also be used to quickly format a range of cells in a worksheet – see the Format as Table gallery in the Styles group.

Table styles will either be applied to:

▶ *The selected range of cells*

Or

▶ *All cells surrounding the selected cell, until a blank row or column is reached.*

When you apply a table style, you are asked if your data range has a header row – column headings at the top of each column. In most cases the cell range will have a header row.

In addition to applying formatting to the cell range, a Table style adds filters to each column heading – these will be discussed in Chapter 9.

If you want the formatting from a Table style, but not the filters, you can still format you cell range using a style, and then click **Convert to Range** in the **Tools** group on the **Table Tools, Design** tab.

To delete a style:

1 Click **Cell Styles** to display the styles.
2 Right-click on the one you wish to delete.
3 Click on **Delete**.

The style will be removed, and any cells that were formatted with it will revert to the Normal style. If the style's formatting remains applied to the cell, it will be because the cell had been formatted by setting options, not by applying a style – you probably created the style by selecting the options applied to the cell.

THE DEFAULT FONT

If you want to change the default font for all new workbooks you can do this separately from creating styles.

1 Click the **File** tab and choose **Options**.
2 Display the **General** category.
3 Select the font and font size required in the **When Creating New Workbooks** area.
4 Click **OK**.
5 Exit Excel and restart it again – the new font settings will be set.

Existing workbooks are not affected.

To duplicate a style:
1 Click **Cell Styles** to display the styles.
2 Right-click on the style you wish to copy.
3 Click on **Duplicate…**
■ A copy of the style will be created.
4 Rename and/or adjust the formatting as required.
5 Click **OK**.
■ To give your worksheets a professional look quickly and easily, use styles to format your cells.

Where do Themes fit in?

We discussed themes in Chapter 4. Themes consist of colour sets, font sets and effects (for shapes, etc.)

When you select a theme, the colours, fonts and effects in that theme will affect any text, data and objects in your file that you haven't formatted locally.

The Theme will affect the colours in the cell styles and table styles, e.g. Heading 1, Heading 2. The colours will also affect the colours in the series formatting on charts, or the shapes you have drawn. The style will control the number format, alignment, protection, borders, etc.

If you have applied *manual* formatting to elements, this formatting will not be affected – it will take precedence over that coming in from a theme.

If you have formatted using the defaults, and used the cell styles – the formatting will update when you choose a different theme (or change the colour, font, and effect options within a theme).

It's a hierarchy – the Themes determine the fonts and colour sets that affect your styles. Changing a theme will affect the styles, shapes and chart formatting in your file. You can choose to control things from the theme level, or from the styles level – or use manual formatting if you want something specific that breaks all the rules.

8.2 Workbook templates

A template is a design on which a workbook or worksheet is based.

It includes things like themes, styles, standard text, formatting and formulas – so all you have to do is add your data.

Up until now, your workbooks have been based on the default template – the Blank workbook. This is the one used to create a new workbook when you start Excel.

If you explore the New Workbook dialog box, you will find that there are many templates to choose from.

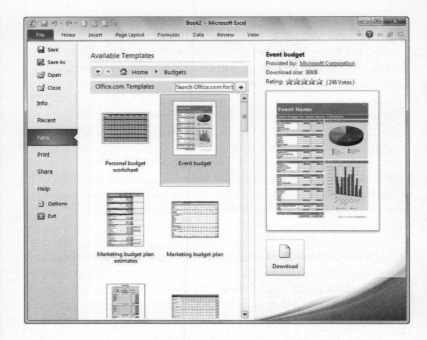

To create a new workbook from any template:
1 Select a template from the list available.
2 Click **Create** (if it is a local template) or **Download** (if it is at Office.com).

You can also create your own templates for workbooks. Using templates can save you time, and also help ensure that workbooks are laid out in a consistent manner.

To create your own template:
1 Create a new workbook (or open an existing workbook).
2 Set it up with the number of sheets and all the standard information, formatting and formulas required, e.g. your company name, logo, column headings, row labels, etc.

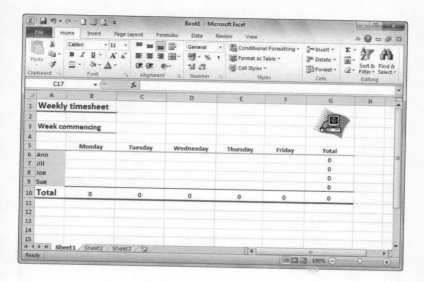

3 Click **File** and then click **Save**.

4 Give your template a name.
5 Select **Excel Template** from the **Save As Type...** list – the Save in: field should change to **Templates** automatically.
6 Click **Save**.
7 **Close** your template file.
■ Excel workbook and worksheet templates have the .xltx file extension.

To create a new workbook using your template:
1 Click **File** and then **New**.
2 At the **New Workbook** dialog box, select **My Templates**.
3 Select your template from the **Personal Templates** tab in the **New** dialog box.

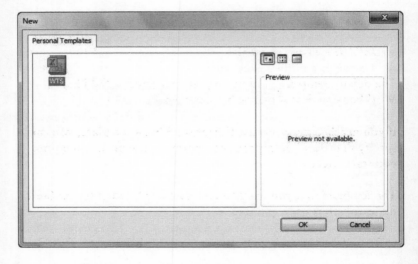

4 Click **OK**. You will have a new workbook that contains all the standard information that you put in your template.
5 Complete your workbook and save it in the normal way (not as a template).

You can reuse your template any time you need to create a new workbook following its layout.

To update your template:

1 Create a workbook using your template.

2 Edit your workbook as required.

3 Save the file as a template, using the same filename as the original.

4 At the prompt, click **Yes** to override the existing template.

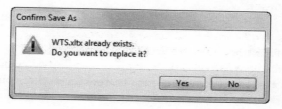

5 **Close** your file.

DEFAULT START TEMPLATE

The default template used when you start Excel is the Blank Workbook (unless someone has changed it).

If you nearly always use a different workbook template, you can specify that the template that you normally use opens each time you start Excel.

The template that you want to use must be placed in the **XLStart** folder which is usually found in

C:\Users\UserName\AppData\Local\Microsoft\Excel\XLSTART

The default workbook template should be called **Book**.

Once you have saved your template to this location, exit Excel and start it again.

The workbook created will be based on your Book template.

If you wish to use another template in the future, or revert back to the blank workbook, you must delete the template from XLSTART (or move it somewhere else).

Note: You may have to display your hidden folders and files to locate the XLSTART folder.

8.3 Worksheet templates

You can also create templates for the worksheets that you add to your workbooks. Previews make them easier to identify.

If you insert a worksheet from the Home tab, Cells group, the *default* worksheet is inserted – when you start using Excel this will be a blank worksheet.

To create a custom worksheet template:

1 Create a workbook consisting of one sheet only.
2 Add any standard text, formatting, formulas, headers and footers, etc. to the worksheet.

To add a preview for display in the Insert dialog box:

1 Click the **File** tab and choose **Info**.
2 Click **Properties** and then **Advanced Properties** in the right panel.

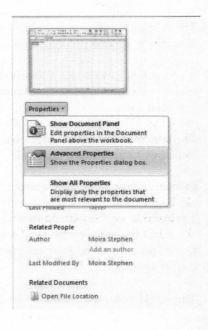

3 On the Summary tab, select the **Save Thumbnails for All Excel Documents.**

4 Click **OK**.
5 Save your file as a template.
6 Close the template.

To insert a worksheet template:
1 Right-click on a sheet tab within your workbook and click **Insert...** on the pop-up menu.
2 Select the template on the **General** tab in the **Insert** dialog box.

3 Click **OK**.

The new sheet will be inserted to the left of the selected one.

DEFAULT WORKSHEET TEMPLATE

The default worksheet template is inserted when you choose Insert, Insert Sheet from the Cells group on the Home tab.

If you want a different default worksheet template the template that you want to use must be placed in the **XLStart** folder which is usually found in

C:\Users\UserName\AppData\Local\Microsoft\Excel\XLSTART

The default worksheet template should be called **Sheet**.

Once you have saved your template to this location, exit Excel and start it again.

The next time you insert a worksheet from the Home tab, the template you saved will be used.

8.4 Chart templates

If you have set up a customized chart layout that you wish to reuse for other charts, you can save it as a chart template (.crtx extension).

To save a chart layout as a template:
1   Select the chart you wish to make into a template.
2   In the **Type** group on the **Design** tab, click **Save As Template**.
3   Ensure that the Charts folder (within the Templates folder) is selected.
4   Give your chart template a name.
5   Click **Save**.

Author's insight
> You can perform standard file management routines on your chart templates from the Insert Chart or Change Chart Type dialog box.

To move or delete a chart template:
1   Display the **Create Chart** dialog box.
2   Click **Manage Templates…**
3   To move the template – drag it to the folder where you want to store it.
4   To delete the template – right-click on it, then click **Delete**. Click **Yes** at the prompt.
5   Close the **Create Chart** dialog box.
■   If you are deleting a chart template, ensure that there are no open workbooks containing charts that are using it.

To apply your template when creating a new chart:
1   In the **Charts** group on the **Insert** tab, click any chart button and choose **All Chart Types…**, or click the dialog box launcher at the bottom right of the group.
2   Select **Templates** at the top of the list on the left of the **Create Chart** dialog box.
3   Click on the template you want to use and then click **OK**.

To apply a template to an existing chart:
1 Select the chart.
2 Click **Change Chart Type** in the **Type** group on the **Design** tab of the Chart tools.
3 Select **Templates** at the top of the list on the left of the **Create Chart** dialog box.
4 Click on the template you want to use and then click **OK**.

CHANGING THE DEFAULT CHART

To set one of your own chart templates as the default chart.

1 Display the **Change Chart Type** dialog box.
2 Select **Templates** at the top of the chart type list on the left.
3 Select the template you want to use as the default chart type.
4 Click **Set as Default Chart**.

Next time you select the cells that you want to create a chart from and press [F11] the chart created will be based on your template.

Author's insight
You will find all sorts of templates (not just Excel) and information on Office templates at http://office.microsoft.com/en-us/templates/default.aspx

THINGS TO REMEMBER

1 *There are features that enable you to automate and customize many of your data and chart formatting routines.*

2 *You can create and edit your own styles.*

3 *Workbooks, worksheets and chart can all be based on templates. Excel offers a range of ready-made templates. These can be customized, or you can create your own templates from scratch.*

4 *You can set any template as the default for a new chart, worksheet or workbook.*

TEST

1 *Give two examples of style types that you will find in Excel.*

2 *Is it possible to modify the styles supplied?*

3 *Is it possible to create new styles?*

4 *How can you quickly apply table style formatting options without the filter in the heading row?*

5 *What is a workbook template?*

6 *What is the difference between a workbook template and a worksheet template?*

7 *If you create a workbook or worksheet template that you want to be your default one where should you store it?*

8 *What formatting elements are controlled by themes?*

9 *To save a chart template you click the Microsoft Office Button and choose Save As... – True or False?*

10 *You can specify that your own chart template is your default chart – True or False?*

9

....

Managing lists and tables

In this chapter you will learn:
* *how to sort data*
* *about filtering data*
* *how to validate data*
* *how to insert subtotals*
* *how to manipulate data using Database functions*

9.1 Terminology

Many of your worksheets will contain lists of data – stock items, customer contact details, exam results, etc. Excel has facilities to sort, find, filter and extract data from these lists. The tasks that you might want to perform on them are often similar to those you would expect to carry out on a database table in Access. Because of the similarity between the working with your data in this way in Excel and in a database, the terminology used is that usually associated with databases.

▶ *Each row is a record.*
▶ *Each column is a field.*
▶ *The column headings are the field names.*

9.2 Sort

The data can be sorted into ascending or descending order. You can perform a simple sort, using the entries in one column only, or a more complex sort, sorting on up to 64 columns at a time.

LISTS FOR SORTING

Give some thought to the lists that you want to sort.

There should be no blank rows or columns inside the area to be sorted.

When you sort data, you will normally want the data surrounding the column you are sorting to be included in the sort – so don't select the column, as this will restrict your sort to that column only. Excel will warn you if you do this. The action is not normally recommended as it can move data away from other data that it is associated with. (If you accidentally sort a column on its own, undo the action – [Ctrl]-[Z] – to put things back as they were, and try again.)

Excel assumes that the first row is a header row (with column labels) and doesn't include it in the sort.

To perform a sort on one column:

1 Select any cell in the column you want to sort on.
2 Click the **Sort & Filter** button in the **Editing** group on the **Home** tab.
3 Choose **Sort A to Z** (for ascending order) or **Sort Z to A** (for descending order).

To perform a multi-level sort (on up to 64 columns at a time):

1 Select any cell within the area you want to sort.
2 Click the **Sort & Filter** button.
3 Choose **Custom Sort…** to open the **Sort** dialog box.

4 Select the main sort column from the **Sort by** list.
5 Set the Sort On option – choose values if you are sorting by text, number or date or time – or cell colour, font colour or cell icon if you are sorting by format.
6 Choose the **Order**.
7 Click **Add level** to add a column for the second-level sort.
8 Repeat steps 4–7 as necessary.
9 Click **OK**.

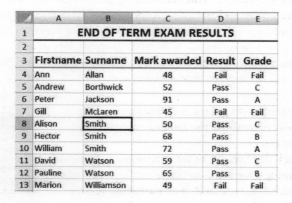

	A	B	C	D	E
1	**END OF TERM EXAM RESULTS**				
2					
3	**Firstname**	**Surname**	**Mark awarded**	**Result**	**Grade**
4	Ann	Allan	48	Fail	Fail
5	Andrew	Borthwick	52	Pass	C
6	Peter	Jackson	91	Pass	A
7	Gill	McLaren	45	Fail	Fail
8	Alison	Smith	50	Pass	C
9	Hector	Smith	68	Pass	B
10	William	Smith	72	Pass	A
11	David	Watson	59	Pass	C
12	Pauline	Watson	65	Pass	B
13	Marion	Williamson	49	Fail	Fail

Note that Excel assumes your list has a header row – the one that normally contains the column labels or field names. If it doesn't, i.e. you want the first row included in the sort, deselect the **My data has headers** checkbox.

To copy a sort level:

1 Open the **Sort** dialog box – click the **Sort & Filter** button and then choose **Custom Sort...**

2 Select the sort row you wish to copy.

3 Click **Copy Level** and then **OK**.

To delete a sort level:

1 Open the **Sort** dialog box.

2 Select the sort row you wish to remove.

3 Click **Delete Level** and then **OK**.

To change the sort level of an item:

1 Open the **Sort** dialog box.

2 Select the sort row you wish to move.

3 Click the Up Arrow or Down Arrow to move the item.

4 Click **OK**.

SORT OPTIONS

You can use Sort to rearrange columns of data as well as the rows. The default Sort options are to sort rows of data from top to bottom, and ignore the case (upper or lower) of your text. To make your sort case-sensitive, or sort columns from left to right rather than rows from top to bottom, use the Sort options.

To sort columns:

1 In the row above (or below) the list, type numbers to show the order you want the columns in.

2 Select any cell in the list you want to sort.

3 Open the **Sort** dialog box.

4 Click **Options** in the **Sort** dialog box.

5 Specify the options required.

	A	B	C	D	E
1	**END OF TERM EXAM RESULTS**				
2					
3	2	1	3	5	4
4	**Firstname**	**Surname**	**Mark awarded**	**Result**	**Grade**
5	Ann	Allan	48	Fail	Fail
6	Andrew	Borthwick	52	Pass	C
7	Peter	Jackson	91	Pass	A
8	Gill	McLaren	45	Fail	Fail
9	Alison	Smith	50	Pass	C
10	Hector	Smith	68	Pass	B
11	William	Smith	72	Pass	A
12	David	Watson	59	Pass	C
13	Pauline	Watson	65	Pass	B
14	Marion	Williamson	49	Fail	Fail
15					

6 Click **OK**.
7 Complete the **Sort** dialog box as required – in this example specifying row 3 as the sort row – and click **OK**.

Once your data has been sorted you can delete the row that contains the numbers that specify the sort order.

	A	B	C	D	E
1	**END OF TERM EXAM RESULTS**				
2					
3	1	2	3	4	5
4	**Surname**	**Firstname**	**Mark awarded**	**Grade**	**Result**
5	Allan	Ann	48	Fail	Fail
6	Borthwick	Andrew	52	C	Pass
7	Jackson	Peter	91	A	Pass
8	McLaren	Gill	45	Fail	Fail
9	Smith	Alison	50	C	Pass
10	Smith	Hector	68	B	Pass
11	Smith	William	72	A	Pass
12	Watson	David	59	C	Pass
13	Watson	Pauline	65	B	Pass
14	Williamson	Marion	49	Fail	Fail
15					

Author's insight

The most common type of sort is one that sorts lists into ascending or descending order – alphabetically or numerically.

You can also sort your data by colour (if you have used different font and/or fill colours) or by icon (if you have used the icon sets in the conditional formatting options).

Explore the Sort dialog box and experiment with the options.

9.3 Filtering

Filtering data allows you to quickly extract subsets of your data from a list. When you filter your data, you end up displaying only those records that meet the criteria that you specify. Note that the sort options are also available in the Filter lists.

To filter using 'equal to', to find a match to a specific value:
1 Select any cell in the data range that you want to filter.
2 Click the **Sort & Filter** button in the **Editing** group, and then click **Filter**.

230

Note that the row containing the headings has filtering enabled on each column.

3 Click the filter arrow in the column you want to use to specify your criteria.

4 Clear the **Select All** checkbox.

5 Tick the checkbox(es) by the criteria you are looking for.

6 Click **OK**.

You can filter on more than one column, e.g. to produce a list of all the males or all the females that pass. You could filter out all the females, then within that subset, filter out those that pass.

Notice the filter indicator in the filter arrow of the columns that you have specified criteria in.

	A	B	C	D	E	F
1	**END OF TERM EXAM RESULTS**					
2						
3	Surname	Firstname	Se	Mark awarded	Grade	Result
10	Smith	Alison	F	50	C	Pass
11	Watson	Pauline	F	65	B	Pass

Filter arrow   Filter indicator

You can filter data using operators other than 'equals to', e.g.

> greater than   < less than   <> not equal to
>= greater than or equal to   <= less than or equal to

To use these, select **Number Filters** or **Text Filters**.

1 Click the filter arrow.

2 Select **Number Filters** or **Text Filters** from the options.

3 Select the operator to use or choose **Custom Filter...**

Filter arrow

4 **Above Average** and **Below Average** filter the list immediately. All other options display a dialog box so you can set up your filter criteria.
5 Complete the dialog box – you specify up to two criteria, and use wild card characters (? and *) if you wish.

To remove filter criteria:
1 Click the filter arrow in the column you want to remove the filter from.
2 Click **Clear Filter** from fieldname.

To remove the filter arrows:
■ Click the **Sort & Filter** button in the **Editing** group on the **Home** tab, then click **Filter**.

The Sort and Filter features are also available on the **Data** tab on the Ribbon.

REMOVING DUPLICATE VALUES

Sort and filter operations are often used to help identify duplicate values in lists of data, with a view to removing duplicates that have been added in error. The Remove Duplicates feature can be used for this task.

To remove duplicates:

1 Select any cell in the list.
2 Click **Remove Duplicates** in the **Data tools** on the **Data tab**.
3 Select the column(s) that you want to check for duplicates.
4 Click **OK**.

Excel will return a summary of how many duplicates have been found and removed.

Note – if you aren't sure whether or not you really want the duplicates removed, copy the list to another location first, and then you can always get the data back easily if you change your mind.

9.4 Tables

Although you can sort and filter data without creating a table, tables make managing and analysing a set of related data easier. The data within the table is managed independently of data in other columns and rows in the worksheet.

Once created, the main benefits in using a table (compared to working with your data as a basic list) are that you can quickly apply formatting and summary calculation features to the table.

When you convert a data range to a table, the Filter feature is automatically activated so you can sort and filter the data in your table quickly.

To create a table:

1 Select the range of data that you wish to identify as a table (or select any cell within the range).
2 Click the **Table** button in the **Table** group on the **Insert** tab (or press [**Ctrl**]-[**T**]).

3 Confirm the data range at the **Create Table** dialog box (edit if necessary).
4 Click **OK**.

You can create several tables on the one worksheet.

	A	B	C	D	E	F
1		END OF TERM EXAM RESULTS				
2						
3	Surname	Firstname	Mark awarded	Grade	Result	
4	Allan	Ann	48	Fail	Fail	
5	Borthwick	Andrew	52	C	Pass	
6	Jackson	Peter	91	A	Pass	
7	McLaren	Gill	45	Fail	Fail	
8	Smith	Alison	50	C	Pass	
9	Smith	Hector	68	B	Pass	
10	Smith	William	72	A	Pass	
11	Watson	David	59	C	Pass	
12	Watson	Pauline	65	B	Pass	
13	Williamson	Marion	49	Fail	Fail	
14						

You can also create a table from the **Home** tab.

1 Select the range of cells you want to become a table.
2 Click the **Format as Table** button in the **Styles** group.
3 Select a **Table Style**.

4 Check the cell range and edit if necessary.
5 Click **OK**.

The Table tools are displayed in the Ribbon.

SORT AND FILTER TABLE DATA

You can sort and filter your table data as discussed above.

9.5 Table styles

Tables can be formatted quickly and effectively using the styles.

To apply or change a table style:
1 Select any cell in your table.
2 Display the **Table Style** options on the **Table Tools Design** tab, or the **Home** tab.
3 Click on the style you want to use.

To enable/disable different elements of the table style:

Select or deselect the options in the **Table Style Options** group:

▶ **Header Row** – *sets the first row as field names with the filter feature enabled.*

▶ **Last Column** – *applies formatting to the last column.*

▶ **Totals Row** – *adds a totals row, where you can perform summary calculations.*

▶ **Banded Rows** – *formats the rows with alternating shading (fill) effects.*

▶ **First Column** – *applies formatting to the first column in the table.*

▶ **Banded Columns** – *formats the columns with alternating shading (fill) effects.*

This next table has Header Row (displayed automatically when you create a table), Totals Row, First Row and Last Column and Banded Rows options selected.

When the Header Row option is selected, the labels in the header row remain visible when you scroll through a long table. They replace the worksheet headers (A, B, C...) so that you always know what the information in your columns is.

	Surname	Firstname	Sex	Mark awarded	Grade	Result
10	Smith	Alison	F	50	C	Pass
11	Watson	Pauline	F	65	B	Pass
12	Watson	David	M	59	C	Pass
13	Williamson	Marion	F	49	Fail	Fail
14	Total			59.9		10

The functions in the Total row are Average for the Mark Awarded and Count for the Result. You can change the function used in any cell by clicking the arrow within the cell and selecting the function required from the list.

The other Table Style options are formatting options.

To create your own table style:
1 Display the Table styles.
2 Click **New Table Style…**
3 Give your table a name.
4 Select the table element to specify the formatting for.
5 Click **Format**.

6 Set up the font, fill and border formats required.
7 Click **OK**.
8 Repeat steps 3–6 for each element.
9 Click **OK** at the **New Table Quick Style** dialog box.

Your style will be displayed at the top of the Table Styles list, in the Custom category.

PRINTING A TABLE

A range of data that has been identified as a table can be printed quickly and easily – without needing to select the cells or identify the range as a print area.

1 Select any cell within the table to activate it.
2 Click the **File** tab, then click **Print**.
3 In **Print** settings: select **Print Selected Table**.
4 Click **Print**.

RESTORE TABLE TO DATA RANGE

To remove the table attribute from a range of data:
1 Click anywhere in the table to activate the Table tools.
2 In the **Tools** group, click **Convert to Range**, then click **Yes** at the prompt.

Author's insight

If you want to keep a check on the number of records displayed as a result of applying a filter keep an eye on the Status bar.

When you filter your list the number of records found will be displayed.

9.6 Advanced Filter

If you want to keep a set of filter criteria for future use, you must use the Advanced Filter option. This requires you to specify the criteria you wish to apply on a separate area of the worksheet (usually above it). The criteria in this range are then applied to your list of data.

The process has two steps:
1 Set up the criteria range.
2 Apply the criteria in the range to your list of data.

To set up the criteria range:
1 Copy the column headings (field names) to a blank area in your worksheet, above the rows you are filtering (insert some blank rows if necessary).
2 Specify the criteria in the rows under the copied headings:
If you enter several conditions in one row, Excel will only return a record where all the conditions in the row are met.
If you enter several conditions in different rows, Excel will return the records that meet any of the conditions specified on any individual row.

The screenshot below gives examples of valid criteria.

	A	B	C	D	E	F	G
	I16			fx			
2							
3	Surname	Firstname	Sex	Mark awarded	Grade	Result	
4	Smith		M	>70			
5							
6	Surname	Firstname	Sex	Mark awarded	Grade	Result	
7	<t					<>Fail	
8							
9	Surname	Firstname	Sex	Mark awarded	Mark awarded	Grade	Result
10				>=60	<=80		
11							
12	Surname	Firstname	Sex	Mark awarded	Grade	Result	
13	Allan						
14	Smith						
15							

▶ The first example will list all Smiths, who are Male and had a mark of over 70.
▶ The second will return all with surnames before T in the alphabet, and who also did not fail.
▶ The third will display all who were awarded a mark between 60 and 80 (inclusive).
▶ The fourth will list those with the surname Allan or Smith.

To apply the conditions set in the criteria range:
1 Select any cell in the list of data that you want to extract records from.
2 On the **Data** tab, click **Advanced** in the **Sort & Filter** group.
3 At the **Advanced Filter** dialog box, select the **Action – Filter the list, in-place** or **Copy to another location**.
4 Check and edit, if necessary, the **List range** – the cells with the data.
5 Set the **Criteria range** – the cells containing your criteria. You must include the field name row as well as all the rows containing the criteria.
6 If you selected **Copy to another location**, set the location for the extracted records. You only need to specify the top leftmost cell of where the results are to appear.
7 Click **OK**.

comeback

If you filtered the list in place, click **Clear** in the **Sort & Filter** group to display all your records again.

SELECT COLUMNS

When you filter in place, all columns are displayed in the result. If you filter to another location, you can specify which columns to include in the copy operation.

To specify the columns:
1 Copy the labels for the required columns to the first row of the area where you plan to paste the filtered rows.
2 When you filter, enter a reference to the cells containing the copied column labels in the **Copy to** box.

The copied rows will then include only the columns for which you copied the labels.

9.7 Data validation

When entering data into a worksheet, you will want to try to ensure, as far as is practicable, that the data is accurate. To help achieve this, you can set up validation rules for any cell or range of cells where you want to check the validity of the data entered.

By default, each cell in a worksheet will accept any value. However, you can limit the range of acceptable entries by setting up validation rules. In our Student Results worksheet, we could set a rule for the data area in the Mark awarded column so that it would only accept values between zero and 100. Anything over 100 or less than zero would not be accepted and an error message would be displayed.

To set a validation rule:
1 Select the cell(s) that you want the rule to apply to (do not include the column heading or any other cells).

2 Click **Data Validation** in the **Data Tools** group on the **Data** tab.

3 On the **Settings** tab, complete the validation criteria fields.

Comeback

4 If you want a message displayed when the cell is selected, enter it on the **Input Message** tab.

5 If you want a specific message to appear when the rule is not met, enter it on the **Error Alert** tab (a default message appears if you don't set up your own).

6 Click **OK**.

comeback

When you select a cell with a validation rule, the **Input Message** will be displayed.
If you enter invalid data into a cell, the **Error Alert** message will be displayed.

Student Results
Enter a value
between 0 and 100

To remove a validation rule from your cells:
1 Select the cell(s) you want to remove the rule from.
2 Click **Data Validation** in the **Data Tools** group.
3 Click **Clear All** and then **OK**.

Creating a drop-down options list

If there is a limited range of possible correct entries for a cell, you can create a drop-down list using the Data Validation feature.

Create a drop-down list from a range of values on the same worksheet:
1 Select the cell that will contain one of the values in your list.
2 Click **Data Validation** in the **Data Tools** group on the **Data** tab.

3 In the **Settings, Allow** field choose **List**.
4 Identify the location of the list in the **Source** field, e.g. Z1:Z4.
5 Select the **In-cell dropdown** checkbox is selected (if you don't select this, you won't get the drop-down arrow next to the cell for data entry).
6 Click **OK**.

You can Autofill the rule down through your column.

At data entry, the user will click the drop-down arrow and select the option required from the list.

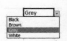

Create a drop-down list from a range of values on a different worksheet:

Type the list of values and name the range (the **Scope** must be **Workbook**).

Then, at step 4 above, in the location field, type =*rangename* rather than the cell addresses.

9.8 Subtotals

Lists of data can be summarized automatically using subtotals. In this example, customers buy stems of flowers from a garden centre. The centre wants to know the total value of orders from each customer over the period. The total of each order is calculated using a formula – see the Formula bar in the illustration.

To display subtotals:
1 Sort the data into ascending order on the field that you want to create subtotals after, e.g. Customer.

H6				f_x =(E6*$I$3)+(F6*$J$3)+(G6*$K$3)						
	A	B	C	D	E	F	G	H	I	J	K

	A	B	C	D	E	F	G	H	I	J	K
1	**Gerry's Garden Centre**								Prices each		
2									Roses	Lilies	Carnations
3	**Order Summary fo December**								£1.00	£1.50	£0.50
4											
5	Order ID	Date	Customer	Town	Roses	Lilies	Carnations	Total Cost			
6	AF001	03/12/2009	Amy's Flowers	Edinburgh	50	60	80	£180.00			
7	AF002	04/12/2009	Amy's Flowers	Edinburgh	60	30	20	£115.00			
8	AF003	07/12/2009	Amy's Flowers	Edinburgh	60	50	90	£180.00			
9	BB001	06/12/2009	Best Blooms	Dalkeith	100	20	30	£145.00			
10	BB002	10/12/2009	Best Blooms	Dalkeith	20	20	20	£60.00			
11	BB003	15/12/2009	Best Blooms	Dalkeith	30	50	70	£140.00			
12	FF100	01/01/2009	Fabby Flowers	Edinburgh	30	10	20	£55.00			
13	FF101	04/12/2009	Fabby Flowers	Edinburgh	22	10	50	£62.00			
14	FF102	08/12/2009	Fabby Flowers	Edinburgh	16	20	30	£61.00			
15	FF103	10/12/2009	Fabby Flowers	Edinburgh	18	22	50	£76.00			
16	FF104	15/12/2009	Fabby Flowers	Edinburgh	16	20	80	£86.00			
17	GT001	03/12/2009	Golden Tulip	Dalkeith	20	20	40	£70.00			
18	GT002	06/12/2009	Golden Tulip	Dalkeith	16	22	30	£64.00			
19	GT003	07/12/2009	Golden Tulip	Dalkeith	20	18	30	£62.00			
20	GT004	08/12/2009	Golden Tulip	Dalkeith	20	24	30	£71.00			
21	GT005	11/12/2009	Golden Tulip	Dalkeith	14	20	70	£79.00			
22	GT006	12/12/2009	Golden Tulip	Dalkeith	14	16	60	£68.00			
23	GT006	16/12/2009	Golden Tulip	Dalkeith	20	30	50	£90.00			

2 Select any cell in the data you wish to create subtotals for.

3 Click **Subtotal** in the **Outline** group on the **Data** tab to display the **Subtotal** dialog box.

4 In the **At each change in:** field, select the item you wish to subtotal on – **Customer** in this example.

5 Select the function from the **Use function:** list (**Sum** in this example).

6 In the **Add subtotal to:** list, tick a box to indicate where to display the subtotal.

7 Select/deselect the checkboxes as required.

8 Click **OK**.

The result is a list showing the data grouped and subtotalled.

	H9	▾	fx	=SUBTOTAL(9,H6:H8)				
1 2 3	B	C	D	E	F	G	H	Pr
	1		**Gerry's Garden Centre**					
	2							
	3	mmary fo December						
	4							
	5	Date	Customer	Town	Roses	Lilies	Carnations	Total Cost
+	9		Amy's Flowers Total					£475.00
+	13		Best Blooms Total					£345.00
+	19		Fabby Flowers Total					£340.00
+	27		Golden Tulip Total					£504.00
−	28		Grand Total					£1,664.00

The outline pane on the left can be used to expand and collapse the level of detail. In the example here, Level 1 = Grand Total, Level 2 = Item Subtotal, Level 3 = Detail. You can display the amount of detail required by clicking the level numbers at the top of the pane.

- You can collapse and expand groups within the list by clicking the Hide [-] and Show [+] buttons in the outline pane.
- To clear the outline, click the **Subtotal** button, then click **Remove All** in the **Subtotal** dialog box.

SUBTOTAL FUNCTIONS

There are 11 subtotal functions, with a different code depending on whether you want to include hidden values in your result:

Function_num (includes hidden values)	Function_num (ignores hidden values)	Function
1	101	AVERAGE
2	102	COUNT
3	103	COUNTA
4	104	MAX
5	105	MIN
6	106	PRODUCT
7	107	STDEV
8	108	STDEVP
9	109	SUM
10	110	VAR
11	111	VARP

It is normally easiest to enter subtotals using the above procedure. The subtotal function is entered automatically to calculate the subtotal for each group and also for the complete range (giving the grand total). Once a subtotal function is entered you can easily edit it directly in the Formula bar if you wish.

To edit the subtotal function:
1 Select the cell that contains the function.
2 Remove the function number from the function in the Formula bar.
3 Right-click, and choose **Pick From Drop-down List**.
4 Double-click on the function to use in your Subtotal.
5 Press [Enter].

Author's insight

If you want to display the number of rows that are displayed as the result of a filter being applied in a cell on your worksheet, you could use the Subtotal function.

For example, if you are filtering rows with the filter information in A2:A800, you could enter the function =SUBTOTAL(2,A2:A800) to your worksheet. The 2 indicates the Count function.

Then, regardless of how you filtered the data on A2:A800, the cell containing =SUBTOTAL(2,A2:A800) would show the number rows (records) displayed in the filtered list.

9.9 Database functions

DCOUNT

DCOUNT looks at a list of values, finds the rows that satisfy specific criteria, and counts them. It's used when you want to count the values that match more than one criterion.

Set up a criteria range – see section 9.6, Advanced Filter.

To insert the DCOUNT function:
1 Select the cell that you want the answer to appear in.
2 Click **Insert Function** in the **Function Library** group on the **Formulas** tab.
3 Select the **Database** category and then **DCOUNT** from the Function list.
4 Click **OK**. The **Function Arguments** dialog box will open. This is where you will specify the details of the function.

5 Enter the range of cells that your list of data fills in the Database field.
6 For the **Field**, enter the column label or number that you want to base the count on (it must be a numeric column).
7 Specify the range that the **Criteria** are in.
8 Click **OK**.

K11 =DCOUNT(A1:E18,3,G1:K2)

	Firstname	Surname	Computing %	Maths %	English %		Firstname	Surname	Computing %	Maths %	English %
1	Firstname	Surname	Computing %	Maths %	English %		Firstname	Surname	Computing %	Maths %	English %
2	Gill	McLaren	45	60	70					>=80	>=80
3	Pauline	Watson	65	88	80						
4	William	Smith	72	76	55		Firstname	Surname	Computing %	Maths %	English %
5	Ann	Allan	48	82	84				>=80		
6	Andrew	Borthwick	52	65	76					>=80	
7	Peter	Jackson	91	49	83						>=80
8	Alison	Smith	50	55	57						
9	Marion	Williamson	49	89	65						
10	Hector	Smith	85	49	74		No of students with				
11	David	Watson	59	66	65		80 or more in Maths and English				3
12	Alice	Graham	65	58	82		80 or more in Computing, Maths or English				10
13	Belinda	Williamson	75	75	45						
14	Colin	Taylor	45	92	88						
15	Derek	Cunningham	80	65	55						
16	Elaine	Nelson	39	77	88						
17	Frances	Watson	57	69	44						
18	Gregory	Young	63	80	70						

USING DATA ENTRY FORMS

A form can make data entry easier for the user than typing data into the worksheet – but the option that allows you to create a quick data entry form is a bit tricky to find!

Display the Form tool:

1 Click the down arrow at the end of the Quick Access Toolbar and choose **More Commands** from the list (this opens the **Customize the Quick Access Toolbar** dialog box).
2 Choose **All Commands** from the **Choose commands from** list.
3 Scroll through the list to find the **Form...** command.
4 Click on **Add** to add the **Form** command to the Quick Access toolbar.
5 Click **OK**. The Form tool will appear on the Quick Access Toolbar.

New Form

To create a data entry form:

1 Select a cell within the list of data and click the Form tool.

2 If all columns have a column heading, a form will be created immediately. If Excel is in any doubt about what cells you want to create a form for it will display a dialog box asking for more information.

New	Adds empty form so you can enter a new record
Delete	Deletes the record you are looking at
Restore	If you edit a record, then change your mind before you leave it, Restore will reset it as it was before you made changes to it.
Criteria	Clears the form so you can enter search criteria – use **Find Prev/Find Next** to move to the next record matching the criteria. (Click the Form button to return to viewing all records.)

DSUM, DMIN, DMAX

Other functions that work along the same principle are DSUM, DMIN and DMAX. In the example below, Excel is used to keep details of orders for cut flowers from retail outlets. Summary data could be produced using the database functions. Experiment with these (following the steps as for DCOUNT, but substituting the appropriate function) to produce summary data.

| File | Home | Insert | Page Layout | Formulas | Data | Review | View |

K15   *fx* =DSUM(A5:F23,"Roses",H5:K6)

	A	B	C	D	E	F	G	H	I	J	K
1			Gerry's Garden Centre								
2											
3	Order Summary for		December								
4											
5	Order ID	Date	Customer	Roses	Lilies	Carnations		Customer			
6	FF100	01/01/2009	Fabby Flowers	30	10	20		Fabby Flowers			
7	GT001	03/12/2009	Golden Tulip	20	20	40					
8	AF001	03/12/2009	Amy's Flowers	50	60	80		Customer			
9	FF101	04/12/2009	Fabby Flowers	22	10	50		Golden Tulip			
10	AF002	04/12/2009	Amy's Flowers	60	30	20					
11	GT002	06/12/2009	Golden Tulip	16	22	30		No of orders from Fabby Flowers			5
12	BB001	06/12/2009	Best Blooms	100	20	30		Roses			
13	GT003	07/12/2009	Golden Tulip	20	18	30		Minimum no ordered by Fabby Flowers			16
14	AF003	07/12/2009	Amy's Flowers	60	50	90		Maximum no ordered by Fabby Flowers			30
15	FF102	08/12/2009	Fabby Flowers	16	20	30		Total no ordered by Fabby Flowers			102
16	GT004	08/12/2009	Golden Tulip	20	24	30					
17	FF103	10/12/2009	Fabby Flowers	18	22	50		No of orders from Golden Tulip			7
18	BB002	10/12/2009	Best Blooms	20	20	20		Roses			
19	GT005	11/12/2009	Golden Tulip	14	20	70		Minimum no ordered by Golden Tulip			14
20	GT006	12/12/2009	Golden Tulip	14	16	60		Maximum no ordered by Golden Tulip			20
21	FF104	15/12/2009	Fabby Flowers	16	20	80		Total no ordered by Golden Tulip			124
22	BB003	15/12/2009	Best Blooms	30	50	70					
23	GT006	16/12/2009	Golden Tulip	20	30	50					

Author's insight

There are lots of Excel database tutorials and tips on the Internet.

Try searching for **excel database functions tutorials** or **excel database functions tips** and explore the results.

THINGS TO REMEMBER

1 *Excel can be used as a database. When data is stored in a table each row is a record, and each column is a field.*

2 *Data can be sorted on a single field and by multi-level sorts.*

3 *Filtering data will extract those record matching certain criteria.*

4 *If a block of data is made into a Table, it can be manipulated and formatted more easily.*

5 *The Advanced Filter allows you to pinpoint data.*

6 *You can set validation rules so that only certain types of data or values are entered into cells.*

7 *Lists of data can be summarized automatically using subtotals.*

8 *There are a set of functions designed for data processing.*

TEST

1 When manipulating Excel data as a database, what terminology can be used to describe a column, column heading and row?

2 What is the maximum number of sort levels in Excel?
   a Three
   b Sixty-four
   c One hundred.

3 Give examples of three different **sort on** options.

4 How can you display the custom filter dialog box?

5 What effect does creating an Excel table have on a range of cells?

6 What is the List Range in an Advanced Filter?

7 Give two examples of how you could use a Validation to help ensure that data is entered accurately.

8 Subtotals are used to summarize lists of data. What must you do to the list before creating the subtotals?

9 The syntax of a database function is:
   a Database, field, criteria
   b Field, criteria, database
   c Criteria, field, database
   d Database, criteria, field.

10 What is a form used for?

10

Macros

In this chapter you will learn:
* *what macros are*
* *how to record, run, edit and delete macros*
* *about making your macros available to all workbooks*

10.1 What are macros?

A macro is a set of Excel commands grouped together so that you can execute them as a single command.

If you perform a task often, but cannot find an Excel keyboard shortcut, or command button, that runs through the sequence you want to use, you should record the commands into a macro. You have then created a 'custom' command.

What could you use a macro for?

▶ *Speeding up routine editing and formatting.*
▶ *Recording the instructions to create a new document using one of your own templates, e.g. your budget or monthly sales figures.*
▶ *Quickly accessing an option in a dialog box that you regularly use.*
▶ *Combining a group of commands you often execute in the same sequence.*

There are two ways to create macros in Excel:

▶ **Recording** – *we will be using this option. You can record any function that you can access through the menus and dialog boxes.*
▶ **Visual Basic Editor** – *you can record powerful, flexible macros using this. These macros can include Visual Basic as well as Excel commands. We will take a brief excursion into the Editor when we discuss editing macros.*

The basic Macro commands (to record, stop recording and play) can be displayed at the left end of the status bar (right-click on the Status bar to customize it if necessary).

You will also find them on the View tab.

1 Display the **View** tab.
2 Click **Macros**.
3 Record Macro...

10.2 Recording your macro

Before you start recording your macro, think through what it is that you want to record. If there are any commands that you're not sure about, try them out first to check that they do what you want to record. Try recording a simple macro that creates a new workbook using one of your own templates.

To create your new workbook, you must:
1 Click the **File** tab and choose **New...**
2 Click **My Templates...** in the **Available Templates**.
3 Select the template.
4 Click **OK**.

The next example uses the template set up in Chapter 8.

To record the macro:

1 Click **Record Macro** on the status bar or in the **Code** group of the **Developer** tab.

2 Give your macro a name – something like *MyTemplate* would be appropriate. Don't use spaces in the macro name – most punctuation characters are also not allowed. If you want to separate words, use the underline character.

3 If you want a keyboard shortcut, click in the Shortcut field and enter the shortcut to use, e.g. [**Ctrl**]-[**Shift**]-[**T**].

4 Select the workbook you want to store the macro in. If you choose the *Personal Macro Workbook*, your macro will be globally available, in every workbook you create.

5 Click **OK**. You will be returned to your worksheet, and the Macro buttons on the status bar and the Ribbon have changed to **Stop Recording**.

6 Work through the steps you want to record.

7 Click the **Stop** button when you've finished. **Recording** has saved the macro automatically.

Make your macros available

If you record a macro in your Personal Macro Workbook, you can access it from anywhere using the keyboard shortcut, or run the macro from the Macro dialog box.

10.3 Playing back your macro

You can play back a macro using the keyboard shortcut (if you specified one) or by using the Play Macro buttons.

To use the keyboard shortcut:

■ Press the keyboard shortcut you recorded, e.g. [**Ctrl**]-[**Shift**]-[**T**] to create your new workbook.

To use the command buttons:

1 Click **Macros, View Macros** on the **View** tab.

2 At the **Macro** dialog box, select your macro from the list.

3 Click **Run**.

The example given is a simple one to illustrate how a macro can be recorded and executed. You will find that macros are especially useful when you have long sequences of commands to work through.

Adding a keyboard shortcut

If you don't give your macro a keyboard shortcut when you create it, or decide to change the keyboard shortcut, you can do so from the Macro options.

1 Click **Macros, View Macros** on the **View** tab.
2 At the **Macro** dialog box, select your macro from the list.
3 Click **Options**....
4 Add, edit or remove the keyboard shortcut.
5 Click **OK**.

10.4 Ideas for more macros

You can record almost anything you want into a macro. Some of the things that you could record into a macro may also be automated in other ways, e.g. Styles. Macros are usually used to carry out a sequence of commands.

If you find that you regularly use a series of commands in the same order, or use an option that is buried deep in a dialog box, macros can help you speed up the way you work.

Try out the following macros to get some more practice. They are all easy to set up.

SETTING UP A HEADER AND/OR FOOTER

If you use the same header and/or footer in many of your workbooks, you could record the sequence of commands into a macro.

DO NOT use the **Header and Footer** button in the **Text** group on the **Insert** tab for this – use the **Page Layout** dialog box.

1 Click **Record Macro** on the status bar or on the **View** tab.
2 Give your macro a name – *HeaderFooter* or similar.
3 Set a keyboard shortcut if you wish, e.g. **[Ctrl]**-**[Shift]**-**[F]**.
4 Select the workbook you want to store the macro in.
5 Click **OK**.
6 Now it's time to add a header and/or footer to your pages. Go to the **Page Layout** tab.
7 Launch the **Page Layout** dialog box – click the launcher at the bottom right of any group on the **Page Layout** tab.
8 Select the **Header and Footer** tab in the **Page Setup** dialog box.
9 Use the **Custom Header** and **Custom Footer** options to set up your header and footer as required.
10 Click **OK** to close the dialog box.
11 Stop recording.

Author's insight

If you want to use a macro to apply formatting, e.g. fill colour/cell border/font colour etc., DO NOT select the cells as part of the macro. Just record the formatting required then stop recording. When you want to apply the formatting, select the cells you want to format *and then* run the macro.

DISCOUNT CALCULATOR

Let's say you offer a discount to your customers based on the amount of their order. You could record a discount calculator into a macro in your Personal Macro Workbook, then access the calculator from any workbook. This macro will:

▶ *Create a new blank worksheet within your workbook.*
▶ *Enter the text and formula to the discount calculator.*
▶ *Protect the sheet so that only the* Amount of Order *details can be entered.*

1 Create a new workbook, or open an existing one.
2 Start to record a new macro. Call it *DiscountCal* or something similar.
3 Set up a keyboard shortcut if you want one.
4 Select the workbook to store the macro in.
5 Click **OK**.
6 Insert a new worksheet.
7 Enter the text and the formula to calculate the discount (in this example 7.5%) and balance due (see below – don't display the formulas).

D16	▾	f_x	
	A	**B**
1	**Total Amount of Order**	
2		
3	**Discount**	=B1*7.5%
4		
5	**Balance Due**	=B1-B3
6		

8 Format the cells to **Currency**.
9 Unlock the cell that will take the *Amount of order* and protect the worksheet (see section 5.10).
10 Stop recording.

10.5 Deleting a macro

As you experiment with setting up macros, you will inevitably end up with some that you don't want to keep. They may not prove as useful as you first thought, or they might not run properly. You can delete any macro you no longer require.

If the macro you want to delete is in the Personal Macro Workbook, you must 'unhide' the workbook before you can delete it.

To unhide a workbook:
1 Click the **Unhide** button in the **Window** group on the **View** tab.
2 Select the workbook – *Personal* in this case.
3 Click **OK**.

If you have displayed your Personal Macro Workbook, you must hide it again once you've deleted any macros you don't want to keep. Do not close it – if you do you won't be able to use the macros that you recorded in the workbook.

To hide the Personal Macro Workbook again:
■ Click **Hide** in the **Window** group on the **View** tab.

To delete a macro:
1 Click the **Macros** button in the **Code** group of the **Developer** tab.
2 Select the macro you want to delete from the list.
3 Click **Delete**.

4 Confirm the deletion at the prompt.

10.6 Editing a macro

I'd suggest you re-record any short macro that has an error in it rather than try to edit it – it will probably be quicker. However, if you have recorded a longer macro or have a minor adjustment to make, it may be quicker to edit it.

The macros you record are translated into Visual Basic – so things may look a bit strange when you first try editing them. But don't worry, if you take your time and have a look through the instructions you'll soon be able to relate your actions in Excel to the Visual Basic code. When editing a macro, be very careful not to delete anything you don't understand, or insert anything that should not be there – you might find your macro no longer runs properly if you do.

If the worst comes to the worst and the macro stops working, you can always record it again.

The Visual Basic code will often have far more lines of code than the number of commands you intentionally recorded. Don't worry about this – some instructions are picked up from default settings in dialog boxes. Just scroll through until you see something you recognize as the line you want to change.

Let's try editing the discount amount in our discount calculator to make it 12.5%. If the discount calculator macro is in the Personal

Macro Workbook, you must unhide the workbook before you can edit it.

To edit the macro:

1 Click the **Macros** button in the **Code** group of the **Developer** tab.
2 Select your macro from the list displayed.
3 Click **Edit**. The Visual Basic code for the macro will be displayed.
4 Scroll through the code to find the area you want to change.

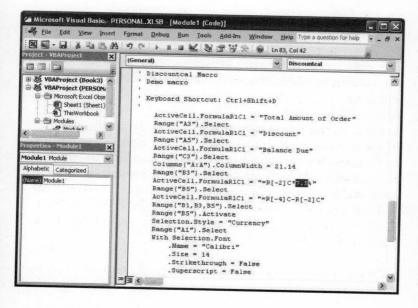

5 Edit as required.
6 Save the changes – click the **Save** tool on the Visual Basic Standard toolbar.
7 Close the Visual Basic window – click the **Close** button at the right of its title bar.

10.7 Saving macros on exit

If you have saved some macros into your Personal Macro Workbook, a prompt will appear when you exit Excel, asking if you want to save the changes to that workbook. If you want to be able to use the macros you have created the next time you use Excel, click **Yes** at the prompt.

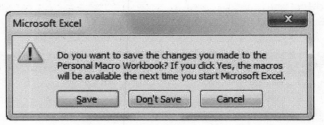

Author's insight

Excel macros can be extremely powerful. To get the most out of them, you will need to record and work on them using Visual Basic (VBA). VBA is outside the scope of this text, but you will find lots of help available on the Internet, in other books, or from your local college/university.

THINGS TO REMEMBER

1 Macros have great potential, as even this brief introduction should to have made clear.

2 You can record any sequence of keystrokes and operations into a macro.

3 Macros can be assigned to keyboard shortcuts for easy access.

4 Macros can be edited using the Visual Basic Editor.

5 Macros saved in the Personal Macro Workbook can be used with any workbook.

TEST

1 *What is a macro?*

2 *Give two examples of what you could use a macro for.*

3 *Where can you save macros?*

4 *Where should you create a macro if you want it to be available to all workbooks that you use?*

5 *Where is the Record Macro button displayed?*

6 *How do you customize the status bar to display the Macro Recording button?*

7 *How can you add, delete or change the keyboard shortcut assigned to a macro?*

8 *Explain how you would delete a macro.*

9 *How can you show (and hide) the Personal Macro Workbook?*

10 *What causes the Saving macros on exit prompt to appear?*

....

Excel with other applications

In this chapter you will learn:
- *the difference between linking and embedding*
- *how to link data in other applications to Excel*
- *how to use Excel data in a Word Mail Merge*

11.1 Get external data

Excel is part of Microsoft Office and integrates very well with the other applications in the suite. If you have the full suite then you have the benefit of being able to use the most appropriate tool for the job, and share your data across the applications.

If you have data held in another application, or a company database, and you want to manipulate it using Excel, you could import it into Excel. This section introduces importing data from external sources.

See 'File Formats that are supported by Excel' in the Help system for full details.

To get data from Access:
1 Select the cell in the top left corner of the range you want to import into (make sure you have enough empty rows and columns for the data).

2 On the **Data** tab, click **From Access** in the **Get External Data** group.

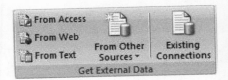

3 Select your data source and click **Open**.

4 Select the table or query from the list displayed.

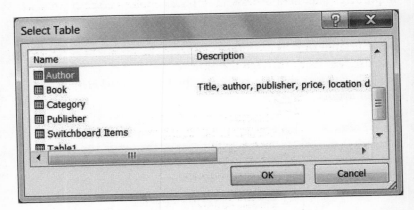

5 Specify how you want to view the imported data, and where you want it placed.

6 Click **OK**.

If you want to import fields from different tables in your Access database, either create a query in Access to pull the fields together, or use Microsoft Query to select the tables and fields required (if importing fields from different tables, the tables should be related in Access).

1 Choose **From Microsoft Query** from the **From Other Sources** list, and work through the wizard.

2 At the **Choose Data Source** dialog box, choose **MS Access Database** on the **Databases** tab and click **OK**.

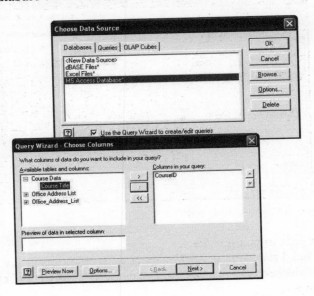

3 At the **Select Database** dialog box, navigate through your folders and select your database and click **OK**.

4 Work through the Query Wizard, selecting your fields, sort order, etc. as you progress through each step.

5 Click **Finish** when you reach the end.

6 Specify how you want to view the imported data, and where you want it placed.

7 Click **OK**.

To get data from the Web:

1 Click **From Web** in the **Get External Data** group.

2 Locate the web page you want to retrieve data from.

3 Click the arrow next to the table(s) you want to import (the cross will change to a tick).

4 Click **Import**.

5 Complete the **Import data** dialog box.

6 Click **OK**.

Import selection arrows

Text files can also be imported easily.

To get data from a text file:

1 Click **From Text** in the **Get External Data** group.
2 At the **Import Text File** dialog box select your file and click
  Import.

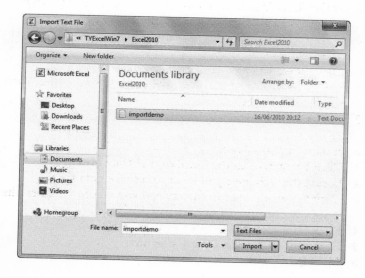

3 Work through the Text Import Wizard.

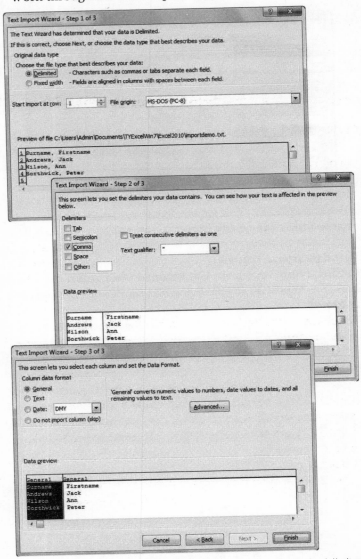

Importing data with the Text Import Wizard – this file used a comma as the delimiter to separate items.

REFRESH

Once you have your data imported into Excel, you can easily keep it up to date with the source file.

To refresh your data:

1 Select a cell anywhere within the data range you wish to update.
2 Click the **Refresh** button in the **External Table Data** group.

To update more than one set of data at a time:

1 Click the arrow at the bottom of the **Refresh** button.
2 Select **Refresh All**.

Refresh options

1 Click the arrow at the bottom of the **Refresh** button.
2 Select **Connection Properties...**
3 Set the **Refresh** options in the **Connection Properties** dialog box.
4 Click **OK**.

If you work with imported data, explore the options associated with this topic using the Help system as necessary.

11.2 Linking vs embedding

Linking and embedding are techniques that enable you to exchange data between Excel and other applications. The key differences between linked and embedded data lie in where the data is stored and how it is updated.

Linking and embedding are techniques that are usually used to get data from Excel into other applications or to create data in other applications using Excel features.

Data held in Access, Word or the Web (for example) that you want to get into Excel is usually inserted using the Get External Data options discussed above.

However, it is easy to copy and paste data from an Access or Word table into an Excel worksheet.

LINKED DATA

Linked data is not stored in the destination file, e.g. your Excel workbook (if the data is coming into Excel) or your Word file (if the data is coming from Excel into Word). It is stored in a file, e.g. a workbook, document or presentation, in the source application (the one in which the data was created). The data is updated within the source application – and those changes are reflected in the destination file, e.g. Excel workbook or Word document to which it is linked.

Advantages of linking data include:

▶ *The destination file, e.g. Excel workbook/Word document is smaller than with embedded data.*
▶ *The data in the destination file reflects the current status of the source data.*

EMBEDDED DATA

Embedded data is stored in your destination file. If it was originally copied from a source file, changes to the source file will not be reflected in the destination file.

However, if you create and edit the data as an embedded object, you have access to all the functions within the source application.

Advantages of embedding data:

▶ *All the data is held in one file.*
▶ *You have access to powerful functions that are not part of the destination application when creating and editing the object.*

The following sections discuss some of the methods you can use to integrate the data across the applications in Office.

11.3 Copy and Paste

You can copy text, data, graphics, charts, etc. from one application to another within the Office suite using simple copy and paste techniques. We will consider how you can copy charts and data from Excel into other applications in the Office suite.

To copy and paste:
1 Start Excel and the application you want to copy the data or chart to.
2 Open the workbook that you are copying from, and the file that will receive the copy.
3 Select the chart or data you want to copy.
4 Click the **Copy** button in the **Clipboard** group on the **Home** tab.
5 Switch to the application you want to copy the data or chart into.
6 Place the insertion point where you want the data or chart to appear.
7 Click the **Paste** button in the **Clipboard** group.

When you copy charts and data in this way, the chart or data is not 'linked' to the original data in the Excel workbook in any way. Should you edit the data in Excel, the data you copied into the destination file remains as it was when you copied it.

You can copy and paste data from Excel into a Word document, a PowerPoint presentation or an Access database. When you copy and paste data into these applications the data is displayed in a table in the destination application.

You can also copy and paste charts from Excel into a Word document or a PowerPoint presentation.

11.4 Linking data

If you want the data that you copy into your file to be kept in line with the data held in Excel, you should create a link to it. You can use the Paste options or Copy and Paste Special to create a link.

To link data:
1 Start Excel and the application you want to copy data to.
2 Select the chart or data you want to copy.
3 Click the **Copy** button in the **Clipboard** group.
4 Switch to the application you want to copy into.
5 Place the insertion point where you want the chart or data to appear.
6 Paste the data using the **Paste** button.
7 Click the **Paste options** button.
8 Choose a link option.

Or

9 Click the arrow under the **Paste** button and choose the link option required from there

Or

Click **Paste Special...**

10 Select the **Paste Link** button.

11 Choose an option from the **As:** list – when you select one a brief description of its effect appears in the **Result** box.

12 Click **OK**.

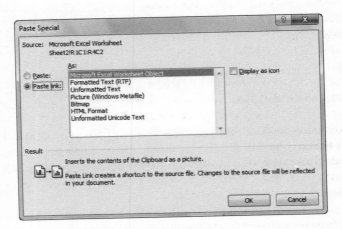

Link the data when it is important that the data in the destination file displays the current up-to-date status of the source file.

When you copy data or a chart and create a link to it in this way changes in the source file in Excel, will automatically update the data in the destination file, e.g. in your Word document or PowerPoint presentation.

11.5 Embedding data

You can copy and paste, or use Paste Special to get data or charts from Excel into a file in Word or PowerPoint. However, if you want data in Word or PowerPoint, and it isn't already set up in Excel (and doesn't need to be), you can insert an Excel worksheet into a Word or PowerPoint file. It will be created and edited using Excel functions.

The Excel Worksheet you insert will be an embedded object.

To insert a Microsoft Excel Worksheet:
1. Place the insertion point where you want the worksheet to appear in your Word document or PowerPoint presentation.
2. Click the arrow under the **Table** button on the **Insert** tab.
3. In Word choose **Excel Spreadsheet**. In PowerPoint choose **Insert Excel Table...**
4. An embedded worksheet is inserted, with the Excel Ribbon displayed.
5. Set up your worksheet as normal.

6 Click anywhere outside the worksheet area when you've finished to return to your Word or PowerPoint file.

7 To edit your worksheet, double-click on it to activate it and the Excel commands.

Author's insight

If you often perform calculations in Word, and don't want to store the data separately in Excel, try using embedded Excel worksheets. The calculation facilities in Word are still pretty limited, and having access to the power of Excel directly from your report, invoice or thesis can be a real time-saver.

11.6 Mail Merge

Data in an Excel workbook can be used as the data document in a Mail Merge in Word. From the worksheets that have been set up in this book, the student results worksheet could be merged into a Word document so that we could send letters out to our students telling them how well they had done in their exams. You could add columns to contain the student address details to the worksheet.

1 The top row of your data should contain the field names. Enter the data that will be merged into your document on the worksheet starting under the field name row.

	A	B	C	D	E	F	G	H
1	Firstname	Surname	Mark awarded	Result	Grade	Address	Town	
2	Gill	McLaren	45	Fail	Fail	10 Gamekeepers Way	Aberdeen	
3	Alison	Smith	50	Pass	C	75 Scott Street	Aberdeen	
4	Ann	Allan	48	Fail	Fail	14 Brunsfield Terrace	Dalkeith	
5	David	Watson	59	Pass	C	15 St Stephen Street	Dalkeith	
6	Andrew	Borthwick	52	Pass	C	25 Potters Row	Edinburgh	
7	Hector	Smith	68	Pass	B	33 Andrew's Walk	Edinburgh	
8	Peter	Jackson	91	Pass	A	61 Milton Park	Glasgow	
9	William	Smith	72	Pass	A	100b St John's Road	Livingston	
10	Pauline	Watson	65	Pass	B	15 High Street	Stirling	
11	Marion	Williamson	49	Fail	Fail	10 Gillespie Cescent	Stirling	
12								

2 In Word, set up your Mail Merge document in the normal
   way. Select your Excel workbook when you open your
   DataSource (Select Recipients).

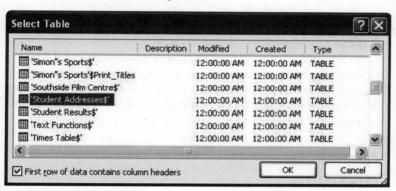

3 Choose the sheet required, or select the named range that
   contains the data you wish to use.
4 Complete the Main Document in Word using the fields from
   your worksheet.

Author's insight

Getting the layout right in your Excel worksheet is critical
to performing a successful mail merge with it. Many of us
inherit Excel worksheets with data destined for a mail merge
operation so check the layout carefully. Mail merge can
actually be performed using any table layout from Office
applications, e.g. a Word table, Excel worksheet, Outlook
Contacts or Access table. The important thing is that the field
names are always in row 1, with the data records starting
in row 2.

If you create a new data file from within Word, a Microsoft Office
Address List will be created (a table within an Access database).

THINGS TO REMEMBER

1 *Excel can import data from Access, the Web and text files.*

2 *If imported data is linked, the source file must always be accessible, but the data will be updated if the original is changed. Embedded data becomes part of the Excel worksheet.*

3 *Data can be imported using the standard Windows Copy and Paste techniques.*

4 *The data in an Excel workbook can be linked or embedded into Word or PowerPoint using Copy and Paste Special.*

5 *An Excel list can be used as the data source in a Word Mail Merge document.*

TEST

1 Name three external data sources from which you can import data into Excel.

2 If you want to import specific fields from an Access table, or from several related tables in Access, what option should you use?

3 Suggest two commonly used delimited options for text files that can be imported into Excel.

4 How can you keep data imported into Excel up to date with the source data?

5 What is the difference between linking and embedding data?

6 What is the potential disadvantage of using a basic copy and paste operation to copy data from and Excel worksheet to a PowerPoint slide?

7 What feature can you use to create a link to source data when you copy and paste?

8 If a Word report contains a table of figures that is linked to an Excel worksheet, where is the data stored – in the report in Word, or in the file in Excel?

9 What are the potential benefits of embedding Excel data in to a Word or PowerPoint file?

10 If you use an Excel worksheet to store data for a mail merge, where should the field names be?

12

....

Excel and the Web

In this chapter you will learn:
- *about hyperlinks*
- *how to send your workbooks by e-mail and fax*
- *about saving files directly to the Internet*

12.1 Hyperlinks

A hyperlink is a 'hot spot' that lets you jump from your workbook to another location – on your own computer, on your company network or anywhere in the world via the Internet.

ADDING HYPERLINKS

You can insert a hyperlink anywhere in your workbook. When you click one, the file that it points to is displayed on screen.

To insert a hyperlink to a file on your system:
1 Select the cell you want to place the hyperlink in.
2 Click the **Hyperlink** button in the **Links** group on the **Insert** tab.

Hyperlink

Links

3 Select **Existing File** or **Web Page** in the **Link to:** options.

4 Enter your display text – this is what will appear in your workbook.

5 Locate and select the file you want to link to.

6 Click **OK**.

To insert a hyperlink to a place within your workbook:

1 Select the cell you want to place the hyperlink in.

2 Click **Hyperlink** in the **Links** group on the **Insert** tab.

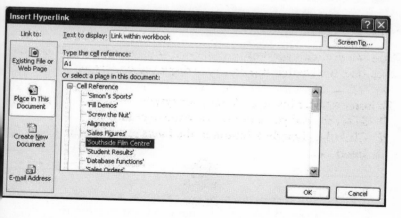

3 Select **Place in This Document** in the **Link to:** options.

4 Enter the text you want on the worksheet in the **Text to display:** field.
5 Enter the cell reference, or select a place from the list.
6 Click **OK**.

To insert a hyperlink to a place on the Web:
1 Select the cell you want to place the hyperlink in.
2 Click the **Hyperlink** button in the **Links** group.
3 Select **Existing File** or **Web Page** in the **Link to:** options.

4 Enter your display text.
5 Type in the address of the page you want to jump to.

Or
6   Click the Magnifying glass button to browse the Web.
7   Locate the page you want to link to.
8   Return to Excel – click **Microsoft Excel** on the Taskbar.
9   Click **OK** at the **Insert Hyperlink** dialog box.

To insert a hyperlink to an e-mail address:
1   Select the cell you want to place the hyperlink in.
2   Click **Hyperlink** in the **Links** group on the **Insert** tab.

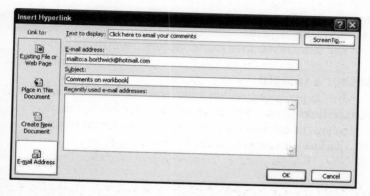

3   Select **E-mail Address** in the **Link
    to:** options.
4   Complete the **Text to display,
    E-mail address** and **Subject** fields.
5   Click **OK**.

To edit a hyperlink:
1   Right-click on the cell that
    contains the hyperlink.
2   Select **Edit Hyperlink...** from the
    menu.
3   Edit the details as required.
4   Click **OK**.

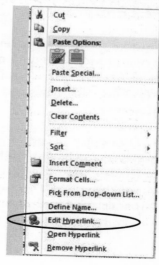

To remove a hyperlink:
1 Right-click on the cell that contains the hyperlink.
2 Select **Remove Link**.

USING HYPERLINKS

To follow the hyperlink:
1 Point to the hyperlink with the mouse.
2 Click the left mouse button.

Once you've jumped to a hyperlink, and then returned to your workbook, the hyperlink field changes colour – usually to violet. This will remind you that you've already used that hyperlink.

Author's insight
When hyperlinking within a file, you might want to add hyperlinks from the places you jump to, back to the place that you jumped from! That way you can return to the hyperlink you clicked easily.

12.2 E-mail and fax

Provided you have a modem, communications software and a service provider, you can e-mail your Excel workbook to anywhere in the world. E-mail is usually very fast – sometimes your message will be delivered almost instantly, other times it may take an hour or so.

You can e-mail an open workbook directly from Excel. The whole workbook can be sent as a file attachment to the message or the current worksheet can be sent, as text, as the body of the message – though this option is only available if Outlook or Outlook Express is your default e-mail application.

To e-mail a workbook from within Excel:

1 Open the workbook you want to e-mail.
2 Click the **File** tab.
3 Select **Save & Send**, and then **Send using E-mail** from the **Save & Send** panel.
4 Choose the send option required from the **Send Using E-mail** panel.
5 Complete the mail message/fax message and send.

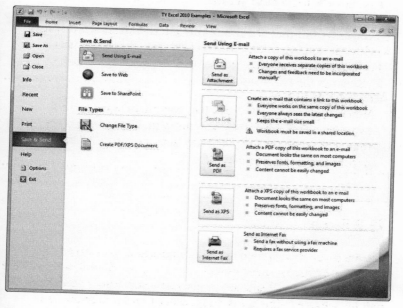

To attach a workbook from within your mail software:

1 Click the **Create a New Mail Message** tool.
2 Enter the addresses in the **To:** field and **Cc:** field if necessary.
3 Type in your subject.
4 Key in your message.
5 Click the **Attach** tool.
6 In the **Open file** dialog box, select the file and click **Attach**.
7 Repeat steps 5–6 if you want more than one file attached.
8 Send your message.

ENCRYPTION

E-mail is not a secure way of transmitting confidential or sensitive data. You should consider encrypting your workbook if you are going to send it via e-mail.

To encrypt your file:
1 Click **File**.
2 Choose **Info, Protect Workbook, Encrypt with Password**.
3 Enter a password – a secure password, e.g. not your name or any word that could be easily guessed. A mixture of text (upper and lower case)/numbers/special characters is best.
4 Click **OK**.
5 Re-enter the password.
6 Click **OK**.

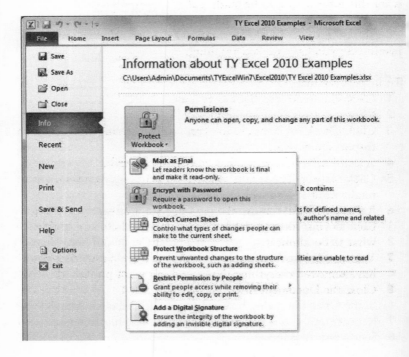

If you don't think you will be able to remember your password, make a note of it and lock it away somewhere safe.

Send the password to the workbook's recipient – *separately* from the workbook – and definitely not in the same e-mail!

12.3 Preparing to share

If publishing data online – whether on an Intranet or the Internet, make sure that you don't publish anything that you didn't mean to.

Things like comments in workbooks, or personal data in the file properties may be useful when developing a file, but you might not want this information to be made public.

You should inspect the file for hidden metadata before publishing – just in case you have missed anything.

To inspect the file:
1 Click **File** to go into Backstage view.
2 Choose **Info** in the panel on the left.
3 Click **Check for Issues** in the **Prepare for Sharing** area and then **Inspect Document**.
4 Select/deselect the areas that you want to check.
5 Click **Inspect**. The results will alert you to any data that you might want to remove.
6 **Remove All** will remove the data in each area – or you can go back to your file and check exactly what is there and decide what to do about it.
7 You can **Reinspect** as necessary until you are happy that you have removed everything that you don't want published.
8 Close the **Document Inspector** when finished.

Author's insight

If you are planning to share your workbook with someone using an earlier version of Excel you could run the Compatibility Checker (a Prepare option in Backstage View) to see if there is anything in your workbook that may give them difficulties. Excel will give details on what the issue is and propose how it will try to resolve the issue.

Depending on what the issue is, you may decide to amend your workbook to overcome the problem area.

ACCESSIBILITY OPTIONS

You can also check your workbook for
accessibility issues. Any issues will be
identified in a panel displayed on the
right of the screen, with suggestions on
how you can fix the problem. You should
review the issues and fix as necessary.

12.4 Office Web Apps

It is now possible to save directly to the Web from this version of Office.

If you work online you can also work on your files using Office Web Apps. Office Web Apps allow you to create and save your files on the Internet so that you can share them with others easily, and work on them from any location with Internet access (so you don't have to keep e-mailing your file to yourself, or saving them to a USB pen when you are on the move). You can also edit files directly online, which helps make collaboration on documents easier.

From Excel 2010 you can save directly to your:

▶ *SkyDrive in your Windows Live account.*
▶ *SharePoint site if your organization has installed and configured Office Web Apps on their SharePoint 2010 site.*

You'll find lot of information about Office Web Apps on the online Help – so if this feature looks useful, check it out.

WINDOWS LIVE

If you have a Windows Live account you can save your files directly to your SkyDrive, and share your files with others.

1 To log in to your SkyDrive from Excel choose **Share, Save to Web** from Backstage view.
2 Click **Sign In** to log in to your Windows Live account.
3 Select the location that you want to save it to on your SkyDrive, and click **Save As**.

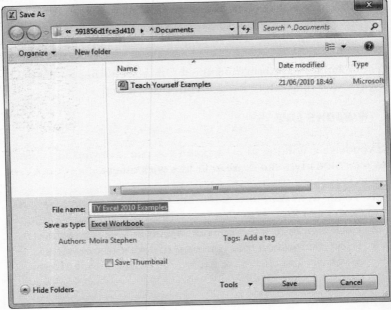

4 Give your file a name, and click **Save**.

Office 2010 is not required to work with Office Web Apps, but Office 2010 programs (Word, Excel, PowerPoint, and OneNote) include commands for saving files directly to SharePoint and Windows Live.

If you access your Windows Live account via the Internet, you will see the files that you have saved on your drive.

If your organization uses SharePoint, you can also save directly to your SharePoint from Excel 2010.

12.5 Research

If you create worksheets where you need to research details, you may find the Resarch feature useful. This enables you to quickly reference information on your computer or online without leaving Excel. The research options include thesauruses, translation tools and access to online reference sites.

It's easy to use and you can customize its setting to suit your own research needs.

1   Click the **Research** button in the **Proofing** group on the **Review** tab.

2 Type in the word or phrase you want to research.

3 Choose your research places from the reference books and sites available.

4 Click the **Go** arrow. The results of the search will be displayed in the **Research** panel.

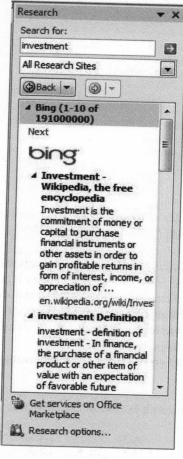

5 Scroll through the panel and read any articles that take your interest.

To customize your Research options:

1 Click **Research Options…** at the bottom of the **Research** panel.

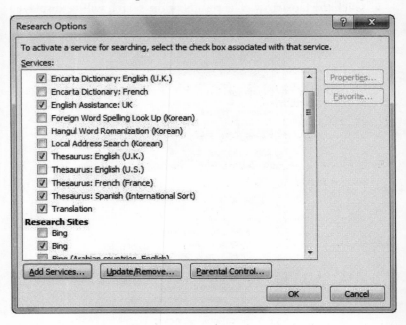

2 Choose **Add Services…** and add any links – you can copy and paste URLs from the Internet.

3 To update or remove services, click **Update/Remove…** and amend your information.

4 Click **OK** to close the **Research Options** dialog box.

THINGS TO REMEMBER

1 *Excel offers you several ways in which you can interact with the wider world.*

2 *You can send e-mail messages and faxes directly from Excel.*

3 *You can create hyperlinks to other files, to places in a workbook and to web pages, adding a user-friendly prompt to them, if wanted.*

4 *You can edit web files and publish your web pages.*

5 *You can search the Internet or your network from within Excel.*

TEST

1 *What is a hyperlink?*

2 *What Link To options are available to hyperlinks?*

3 *In the Insert Hyperlink dialog box what field contains the text that will be displayed on the worksheet?*

4 *How do you edit an existing hyperlink?*

5 *What do you have to do to activate a hyperlink, so that it takes you to wherever it is pointing?*

6 *Suggest two ways in which you could distribute a workbook electronically.*

7 *To protect the security of your data when sending it via e-mail, what should you do?*

8 *What feature helps ensure that you don't publish anything you didn't mean to?*

9 *Identify two Internet locations you can save to directly from Excel.*

10 *Is it possible to edit an Excel workbook stored online using Office Web Apps?*

Taking it further

If you've mastered half of what's in this book, you are well on the way to becoming a proficient Excel user. If you are getting to grips with most of it, you are doing very well indeed.

You'll find lots of information on Excel on the Internet, in addition to the Help menu option Microsoft Office Online that takes you to their website.

You could also try searching the Web for sites that provide information on Excel. Try entering "Microsoft Excel" + "Software Reviews" into your search engine. You should come up with several sites worth a look.

If you would like to join a course to consolidate your skills, you could try your local college, or search the Internet for on-line courses. Most courses cost money, but you may find the odd free one – try searching for + Excel + tutorial + free.

Good Excel skills are useful on many levels – personal, educational and vocational. Now that you have improved your Excel skills, why not consider going for certification? The challenge of an exam can be fun, and a recognized certificate may improve your job prospects. There are a number of different bodies that you could consider.

You may want to consider Microsoft Certified Application Specialist (MCAS) exams or ECDL (European Computer Driving Licence) – basic or advanced certification. Or, if you feel more ambitious, how about other Microsoft Certified Professional exams?

Visit http://www.microsoft.com/learning/en/us/certification/mbc. aspx#tab2 for information on MCAS certification or http://www. ecdl.com for information on ECDL.

Answers

Chapter 1

1 See page 4.
2 i) [**Ctrl**]-[**F1**]
   ii) [**F1**].

Chapter 2

1 (b)
2 (e)
3 Create New file; Save As; Open a file; Save
4 [Ctrl]-[G] or [F5]
5 Hold down [Ctrl] and click on each cell.
6 Number in cell – column not wide enough to display number (widen column or format number to fit)
7 Bold, alignment (centre, left, etc.), font, font size
8 Currency, percentage, comma
9 (c)
10 (b)

Chapter 3

1 FILL colour adds a colour to the cell background, FONT colour formats the text/numbers within the cell.
2 Cell styles will let you apply several formats, e.g. size, colour, border **quickly**, and helps ensure that similar cells are formatted **consistently** within and across workbooks.

3 Conditional formatting.
4 When you want to scroll to see part of a worksheet that is off the screen, but you don't want to lose sight of the row and/or column headings.
5 At the top of the vertical scrollbar and to the right of the horizontal one.
6 Print area.
7 True.
8 False – it doesn't print.
9 Gridlines are usually displayed to mark columns and rows clearly on the screen when you are working on your worksheet – borders are usually added to help format the worksheet so that different areas of it are clearly identifiable.
10 In the header or footer.

Chapter 4

1 To the left of the sheet tabs.
2 To display your data in a clear, unambiguous way.
3 Colours, fonts and effects.
4 3.
5 Excel Options, General category.
6 Rename, Add, Delete, Move, Copy, etc.
7 False.
8 Group sheets.
9 Tab colour.
10 Protect the workbook structure – Review tab, Changes group.

Chapter 5

1 =Max(C2:E2)
2 =Min(C8:E8)
3 =Average(C11:E11)
4 =Max(C2:C18)

5 =Min(D2:D18)

6 =Average(E2:E18)

7 =Count(C2:C18) – or similar function for column D, E, F, G or H (or CountA(A2:A18) – or similar on column B)

8 =Max(C2:E18)

9 =Min(C2:E18)

10 =Average(C2:E18)

Chapter 6

Questions 1–5.

	A	B	C	D	E
1	Today's date	=TODAY()			
2	**Stock Clearance Sale**				
3	**Item**	**No in stock**	**Put in sale?**	**Rec Retail Price**	**Sale Price**
4	Desks	10	=IF(B4>=10,"Yes","No")	750	=IF(C4="Yes",D4*50%,D4)
5	Tables	6	=IF(B5>=10,"Yes","No")	950	=IF(C5="Yes",D5*50%,D5)
6	Chairs	15	=IF(B6>=10,"Yes","No")	225	=IF(C6="Yes",D6*50%,D6)
7	Sofas	9	=IF(B7>=10,"Yes","No")	925	=IF(C7="Yes",D7*50%,D7)
8					
9	**Number of items in sale**		=SUMIF(C4:C7,"Yes",B4:B7)		
10					
11	**Summary of stock held**		=(CONCATENATE(B4," ",A4," @ £",D4," (",$D$3,")"))		
12			=(CONCATENATE(B5," ",A5," @ £",D5," (",$D$3,")"))		
13			=(CONCATENATE(B6," ",A6," @ £",D6," (",$D$3,")"))		
14			=(CONCATENATE(B7," ",A7," @ £",D7," (",$D$3,")"))		

6 Loans = pmt; rate; pv Investments = fv; npv.

7 IF (usually nested IFs).

8 A Data Table, Goal Seek and Scenarios.

9 Pivot Table.

10 By position and by formula.

Chapter 7

1 Rectangle.

2 Ctrl.

3 [F11].

4 Line, bar, column, pie, Sparklines (a kind of chart), etc.

5   Overlap is the amount that each data series overlaps with on a chart, gap is the space between each group of data series.
6   Select the chart and then print (if it is embedded) or put chart on a separate chart sheet and print from there.
7   Hold down [Shift] as you draw it (using rectangle shape).
8   Group – combines several selected shapes into one object. Ungroup – separates a grouped objects into the individual shapes again.
    Regroup – groups individual shapes that have been ungrouped back into one object.
9   It hides and shows the selected shape.
10 Rotate – moves the shape around its centre by a specific amount (degrees); Flip – rotates the shape by 180° horizontally or vertically.

Chapter 8

1   Cell, Table.
2   Yes.
3   Yes.
4   Apply the table style required and then click Convert to Range in the Tools group on the Design tab of the Table tools.
5   A file that contains layout, formatting and standard elements in a workbook, and from which you can then create a workbook into which you type your data. Templates are used to help speed up the production of workbooks and standardize the presentation of data.
6   A workbook template can consist of many worksheets, and is used when creating a working workbook. A worksheet template consists of one worksheet only, when can be added to any workbook as and when required.
7   XLStart folder.
8   Colour, font and effects.
9   False – use Save as Template – Chart tools, Design tab, Type group.
10 True – from the Insert or Change Chart Type dialog box.

Chapter 9

1 Column = field, column heading = field name, row = record.
2 (b) 64
3 Values, cell colour, font colour, cell icon
4 Toggle the column heading filter, then choose **Number Filters** (or **Text Filters**) from the filter list. Any option that leads to a dialog box will display the Custom Filter dialog box.
5 It switches on the filter, formats the cells and allows you to manipulate the list independently from the rest of the worksheet. It also makes printing the cells within the table easier as you can print the table (without having to select the cells or set a print range).
6 The range of cells you are extracting data from (the database).
7 You can use it to limit the range or permitted values, or you could use it to display a drop-down list of acceptable data.
8 Sort it on the column you want to summarize data for.
9 (a) database, field, criteria.
10 Data entry and edit.

Chapter 10

1 A macro is a set of macro commands, grouped together into a named sequence.
2 Combining a group of commands you often execute in the same sequence; speeding up routine formatting and editing.
3 Any open workbook, a new workbook or the Personal Macro Workbook.
4 Personal Macro Workbook.
5 Status bar.
6 Right-click on the Status bar, select Macro Recording.
7 View tab, Macros (Macros group), View Macros, select the macro in the list, click Options..., update keyboard shortcut, click OK.

8 View tab, Macros (Macros group), View Macros, select the macro in the list, click Delete.
9 View tab, Unhide/View tab Hide.
10 This appears when you exit Excel after you have added new macros to the Personal Macro Workbook.

Chapter 11

1 Access, Web, Text.
2 From Other Sources, or From Microsoft Office Query.
3 Tab and comma.
4 Refresh.
5 The difference lies in the location of the data, and the way in which the data is updated.
6 The data on the slide will remain as it was when it was pasted – it will not be kept up to date with changes that happen in the Excel file. There may be times that this is a disadvantage, at other times you may want to data to remain as it was when it was copied/pasted.
7 Paste Special.
8 In Excel.
9 All the data is held in one place, e.g. the Word or PowerPoint file – but you have Excel features available when you create and edit the data.
10 In the first row of the Excel worksheet.

Chapter 12

1 A 'hotspot', that when clicked, takes you to another place in your workbook, another workbook or file, the Web, etc.
2 Existing File or Web Page, Place in the Document, Create New Document or E-mail Address.
3 Text to display.

4 Right-click on it and choose Edit Hyperlink...
5 Click on it.
6 E-mail or fax.
7 Encrypt the file.
8 Inspect Document.
9 SkyDrive and SharePoint.
10 Yes.

Index